REAL-LIFE MIRACLES . . . FROM PRAYER

- **Prayer miraculously heals a child's crushed hand.** . . . Discover what happened when X rays showed a young girl's hand was completely crushed, then her mother began to pray. . . .

- **A dying child whom medicine couldn't cure.** . . . Her parents were doctors, but their medical knowledge was useless, so in desperation they made one incredible phone call. . . .

- **A church prayer group heals a broken arm.** . . . After a fall at a roller-skating rink, this woman's arm had broken in two places, but before she let the doctors set it, she contacted her church's prayer group with astounding results. . . .

- **A family who prayed their mom back from a fatal coma.** . . . The doctors said the 48-year-old woman would never recover, but their children and husband refused to believe it, and they began to pray. . . .

DISCOVER THESE REAL-LIFE STORIES AND MORE IN . . .

The Power of Prayer to Heal and Transform Your Life

The Power
of Prayer to Heal
and Transform
Your Life

by

Sherry Hansen Steiger

A SIGNET VISIONS BOOK

SIGNET
Published by the Penguin Group
Penguin Putnam Inc., 375 Hudson Street,
New York, New York 10014, U.S.A.
Penguin Books Ltd, 27 Wrights Lane,
London W8 5TZ, England
Penguin Books Australia Ltd, Ringwood,
Victoria, Australia
Penguin Books Canada Ltd, 10 Alcorn Avenue,
Toronto, Ontario, Canada M4V 3B2
Penguin Books (N.Z.) Ltd, 182–190 Wairau Road,
Auckland 10, New Zealand

Penguin Books Ltd, Registered Offices:
Harmondsworth, Middlesex, England

First published by Signet, an imprint of Dutton Signet,
a member of Penguin Putnam Inc.

First Printing, September, 1997
10 9 8 7 6 5 4 3 2 1

REGISTERED TRADEMARK—MARCA REGISTRADA

Printed in the United States of America

I give constant thanks to the Living God for guiding me through many times of darkness and pain with the realization that such times are merely challenges and opportunities for spiritual growth and strengthening. There is always a ray of hope through faith and belief in the lessons and purpose in life.

To my Melissa, who experienced with me many of these challenges, but *through* them, grew not only in stature but into a most remarkable guiding light and helper to others.

To my other children, Erik (in spirit), and stepchildren: Julie, Kari, Steve, and Bryan—and their families. To my parents, Lorraine and Paul Lippold, my Aunt Del, my sister-like Aunt Cheryl, my Grandma and Papa Johnson (in spirit), and the rest of my family, who taught me spiritual values and the importance of putting God first in my life.

And especially to my mentor, best friend, helpmate and life partner—my husband, Brad, I dedicate this book. Daily, our prayers go out to all of you.

Special gratitude goes to my editor,
Danielle Perez, and agent, Agnes Birnbaum,
for their patience and encouragement.

Contents

Contents

Lord, Help Me to Help Others

Please help me think of all
   the nicest words that I can say,
The nicest favors I can do
   to brighten up a day.
Please help me be as gentle and as kind as I can be
   Whenever someone turns
     for warmth and thoughtfulness to me.
Please help me gladly listen, and help me truly care
   Whenever someone turns to me
     with special things to share.
Please help me to be deserving
   of lasting faith and trust,
Help me to be generous, always fair and just.
   Whenever someone turns to me,
     please help me to come through. . . .
The way that You come through for me
   each time I turn to You.

—ANONYMOUS

My prayer for you is that you will over-
flow more and more with love for others,
and at the same time keep on growing in
spiritual knowledge and insight.
—PHILIPPIANS 1:9

1

What Is Prayer?

It is the night of the Passover. A peasant is rushing to finish his work in the fields so he can attend the holy service. But, alas, the sun drops and it is darkness when no travel is permitted. Next day the rabbi spots him and asks him where he's been.

"Oh, Rabbi, it was terrible—I was stuck in my fields after dark and had to spend the night there."

"Well," says the rabbi, "I suppose you at least recited your prayers."

"That's the worst of it, Rabbi, I couldn't remember a single prayer."

"Then how did you spend the holy evening?" asks the rabbi.

"I could only recite the alphabet and pray that God would rearrange the letters."

This is a very old parable retold.

My husband and I have always said that while we are on "schoolhouse" earth, it seems there are "oh, so many lessons" to learn. So often, the more we learn, the more we feel we are only in kindergarten in this school, and we each might spell out the name of God in our own language, yet we all use the same elements—kindergarten blocks.

Each of us ultimately needs to discover why we are here, who we really are, where we are going in life, and what is our purpose? Each of us longs for that "something more"—that spiritual connection that carries all the way through the beginning to the end and back again. No matter what name we call God it is always *prayer* that takes us *to* God. Prayer is the link to the way we talk to God, and therefore, find the answers to *everything* else.

The Lord is nigh unto all them that call upon Him, to all that call upon Him in truth.— PSALMS 145:18

Catherine of Siena experienced holy spiritual visions. Following one of her divine experiences she wrote, "And what shall I say? I will stutter 'A . . . A,' because there is nothing else I know how to say." I can relate to that, as I, too, have been blessed with spiritual experiences that have come from the depths of prayer, and often after reaching the depths of despair. There are no words to describe such experiences. They are "ineffable," yet in the mind of the experiencer they are more vivid than reality; and any attempt to share the kind of sacred sight and sounds with others only leaves one completely frustrated as the words pale and seem incapable of even touching a fraction of the blessing.

In the book of Revelation in the Bible, we are told that no one knows the name of God. In the Old Testament, the name of God was too holy and sacred to be repeated. It was forbidden to even try. In fact, it was criminal blasphemy to pronounce the ancient name of God. The Lord God Jehovah or Yahweh was the closest allowed.

There are at least a hundred names of God, which are really *characteristics of God* . . . or *aspects* of God. God is a concept too large for our finite minds to comprehend. In essence, God will remain a mystery while we spirits dwell in human flesh. We have to *know* God from a *spiritual* and heartfelt perspective. God is spirit, therefore, must be worshiped in Spirit and Truth. We are told that in God there is no male or female, no north or south, no east or west. God is omniscient, God is omnipresent, Omnipotent. God is all. All is God. God is in all. God is love.

Some of us, however, are bogged down with many questions. What do we call God? Do we visualize a "father time" image? Where do our prayers go? How can God have time to hear everyone's prayers? Why would God care about me? In essence, this, too, remains a mystery to the questioning mind, although quantum physics and new discoveries make it impossible in my mind for anyone *not* to believe in God.

There exists a kind of separatism and blame that often comes *because* of trying to define the "name of God." If someone else calls "God" by a different name—different from the one we use or are used to hearing—then they think that this "different name" must mean these people are worshiping idols or false gods or "other" gods! I have found from personal observation and experience with people around the world that it is the same One God whom most of us worship. Maybe to get rid of the confusion, we should go back to not pronouncing the name of God—or become less concerned with name-calling.

God, whether called Allah, Divine One, Great Spirit, Holy of Holies, Great Mystery, King of Kings, Lord of Lights, Light of Lights, Lord of Lords, Lord, Most High, Mother/Father God, or Supreme Spirit, Abba, One God or One Spirit—is God. We are not to judge another's path to God, or insist they use our language or rituals. The *real work* and task at hand is to find our own.

Pray without ceasing.—1 THESSALONIANS 5–17

Gail Ramshaw-Schmidt is president of the Liturgical Conference and the recipient of a Rockefeller Brothers Theological Fellowship. In her book, *Letters for*

God, she writes: "Always we must be learning to pray: and lest our prayers and our liturgies smother the God they address, always our religious imagination must be quickened. For even our richest and deepest language of faith—the images of the Psalms, the words of the gospel, the symbols of the liturgy—can only hint at the reality of God."

Then, when we get to the personal experience of God, we are back to the "A. . . .," "what can I say"—back to the ineffable, where there is *no definition* of God or of the communication between—through prayer. And that brings us back to who God says He is. . . . *I AM THAT I AM . . . BECAUSE I AM.*

⁓

God is spirit and they that worship him in
spirit and truth. (pneuma . . . meaning
current or breath of air . . . vital principle or
that which breathes into the human . . .
the superhuman spirit of life . . . spiritual
dimension like angel/ghost, etc. . . .
[AKA: Holy spirit.]—JOHN 4:24

⁓

As the nineteenth-century philosopher William James expressed, if one were asked to characterize the life of religion in the broadest and most general terms possible, one might say that it consists of the belief that there is an unseen order, and that our supreme good lies in harmoniously adjusting ourselves thereto.

James stated, "Scientists tell us that, without the presence of the cohesive force amongst the atoms that comprise this globe of ours, it would crumble to pieces and we would cease to exist. And even as there is cohesive force in blind matter, so must there be in all things animate, and the name for that force is *LOVE*. We notice it between father and son, between brother and sister, friend and friend. But we have to learn to use that force among all that lives, and in the use of it consists our knowledge of God."

Prayer takes the mind out of the narrowness
of self-interest, and enables us to see the
world in the mirror of the holy."—ABRAHAM
JOSHUA HESCHEL, *Modern Spirituality*

Albert Einstein believed in the power of prayer. As one of my favorite clergy persons, Dr. Eric Butterworth, states, "Einstein refers to one law which contains the sum of all that mathematics and physics have proved true about the Universe. He says that this law is a positive force for good and that we can tune in and be a part of the infallibly perfect working by the power and thought of prayer." We are reminded here that Jesus taught that "God is Spirit and they that worship Him must worship in spirit and truth."

In his excellent book, *Discover the Power Within You*, Dr. Butterworth defines the purpose of prayer: "The most important purpose of prayer is lifting ourselves to a high level of consciousness where we can be conditioned in mind and body with the all-sufficient life, substance, and intelligence of God."

⌒

> Your cravings as a human animal do not
> become a prayer just because it is God you
> ask to attend to them.—DAG HAMMARSKJÖLD

⌒

In describing what prayer is not, Butterworth echoes my exact sentiments when he says, "We must work to alter the concept of God as the 'answer man,' the 'super-doctor,' 'the divine warehouse,' and the concept of prayer as the great 'spiritual slot machine.' Do not pray because you think you should pray. Do not pray only to heal your arthritis or to get a better job. You will get your reward, but you will not experience the 'meat which endureth.' That is the great need. Pray to reestablish your contact with the divine power, and 'all these things shall be added unto you.' "

What Prayer Is Not

Jesus not only gave us a formula for prayer but he made it clear what prayer is not when addressing the *Sermon on the Mount:*

> Take heed that ye do not your righteousness before
> men, to be seen of them; else ye have no reward with

your Father who is in Heaven. When therefore thou
doest alms, sound not a trumpet before thee, as the
hypocrites do in the synagogues and in the streets,
that they may have glory of men. Verily I say unto
you, They have received their reward. But when thou
does alms, let not thy left hand know what thy right
hand doeth; that thine alms may be in secret: and
the Father who seeth in secret shall recompense thee.
And when ye pray, ye shall not be as the hypocrites:
for they love to stand and pray in the synagogues
and in the corners of the streets, that they may be
seen of men. Verily, I say unto you, They have received their reward. But thou, when thou prayest,
enter into thine inner chamber, and having shut thy
door, pray to thy Father who is in secret, and thy
Father who seeth shall recompense thee.

—MATTHEW 6:1–6

Here, Jesus tells us what prayer is not. It is not a
matter of using the proper words, the right order or
type of prayer for different occasions . . . it is a matter
of the very heart and sincerity of the pray-er. Prayer
is not for show. As Dr. Butterworth states, "Man is
a thinking being, and the mind is the connecting link
between God and man. Jesus is saying that prayer is
not a matter of words or of outer forms. It is a matter
of consciousness, of concentrated, rightly directed,
spiritually oriented positive thinking. The law is, 'As
he thinketh in himself so is he.' "

"In secret" not only means not to pray for attention or to show off your intellect or "spiritual or theo-

logical knowledge." But in directing us to go behind closed doors, Jesus is also describing this nonmaterial force that cannot be seen. We cannot "see" our thoughts. However, there is *nothing* that exists that was not *first* . . . a thought, which was invisible!

Jesus clearly tells us in many other places that we are responsible for our every thought and that we must learn to master them in thinking only about that which is righteous, good and holy.

> Think on whatsoever things that are true.
> Think on whatsoever things that are honest.
> Think on whatsoever things that are just.
> Think on whatsoever things are pure.
> Think on whatsoever things are lovely.
> Think on whatsoever things that are of good report.
> Think on virtue.
> Think on praise.   —PHILIPPIANS 4:8

The outward acts and ritual are not wrong. They have their place and serve their function. They can very much direct our attention toward that which we want to be. But if we are deluded into thinking that it is *through* the outward acts of saying prayers by rote, reading prayers from books, wearing ceremonial garb, or performing various ritualistic functions, including attending religious services faithfully or tithing faithfully . . . that will make us "holy in the sight of God," we are mistaken.

Science tells us that in order to change an element,

the very nucleus must be changed. I believe that rituals and recitation can be instrumental in "getting there" . . . but it is the goal to get to the very heart of the matter. Our hearts . . . are the "heart of the matter"—to direct our thoughts, mind, and feelings to become pure and focused—in alignment with God.

Prayer is how we converse with God. Prayer is how we get in touch with the essence of who we are. Prayer is trying to bridge the two—our inner and outer self—with God. It is through these conversations with God without (Spirit) and God within (that Spirit within us)—that I believe we can find out *who we really are* and to pray for help to redirect ourselves to what we want to become. Through these conversations we can find our way to that of the "New man or woman" in Spirit, in God, and therefore, to gradually change our very selves. To me, that is the secret of prayer. Prayer can heal and transform our very essence to that which we wish to become!

⌒

The world may doubt the power of prayer.
But the saints know better.
—GILBERT SHAW

⌒

The Old Testament is full of beautiful illustrations of the many kinds of prayer. There are prayers of frustration and anger as well as prayers of praise and thanks, prayers of discouragement and depression, prayers of affliction and burden, prayers to God to take one's life, prayers for healing and deliverance and even prayers for revenge. All kinds of prayer are okay, because they help us to get in touch with our inner feelings in these conversations with god.

One of the most significant illustrations of prayer, yet one of the least dealt with in our day, is that of prayer being used in a praying contest.

The Praying Contest

The ninth-century Hebrew prophet and reformer, Elijah (Eliyahu ha-Navi, in Hebrew), is one of the most captivating of the priests or sages of the Old Testament. Elijah is described as having appeared mysteriously, from an unknown background. He fought as a soldier of the Lord against heathen gods. He championed the downtrodden, performed many astounding miracles and then *vanished* up into heaven in a blazing chariot of fire.

Halfway through the reign of what the Bible calls the most wicked of the Hebrew kings, in approximately 864 B.C., is the first mention of Elijah. This wicked king was Ahab, son of Omri in the northern kingdom of Israel. Both Omri and son Ahab allowed shrines to be built to the Baal god and to the fertility goddesses. A pagan temple was built in the hilltop palace and capital of Samaria. Ahab's' wife, Jezebel, maintained 450 priests or "false prophets" of Baal and 400 prophets of Asherah as part of her own household.

The Israelite priests and prophets who objected to these pagan ways were suppressed or driven out. Then appears Elijah. Elijah of Tishbite, an inhabitant of Gilead (an Israelite province east of the Jordan river). Elijah came with a message for the people . . . he cried out: "As the Lord the God of Israel lives, before whom I stand, there shall be neither dew nor rain these years. . . ." (1 Kings 17:1).

After Elijah made his prayer and prediction for the land and the heathen people . . . he escaped. In the third year of this punishment from God that Elijah relayed to the people, Elijah was again told by God that the drought was about to break. God told him to go again to King Ahab.

The king had been searching for Elijah, so when Elijah's return was messengered to him, he hurried out to meet Elijah. "Is it you, you troubler of Israel?" (1 Kings 18:17). Elijah responded by telling Ahab that it was not him but it was Ahab himself who was bringing God's wrath upon Israel for worshiping false idols—forsaking God and worshiping Baal.

Elijah demanded that an assembly of the people be called on top of Mount Carmel for a contest between the God Jehovah and the god Baal. Elijah was going to have all witness a contest between the priests of Baal, who had been brought to Samaria from Phoenicia by Queen Jezebel. Elijah said to the crowd before the king, "How long will you go limping with two different opinions? If the Lord is God, follow him; but if Baal, then follow him." (1 Kings 18:21). Then Elijah proposed the following contest:

Elijah told the priests of Baal to cut up a bullock and lay the pieces on firewood. Elijah would do the same. They would see which divinity would send down fire to consume the sacrifice.

From morning until noon the priests of Baal leapt around their altar and cried out their prayers to Baal, but there was no answer. Elijah taunted them, "Cry aloud, for he is a god; either he is musing, or he has gone aside, or he is on a journey, or perhaps he is asleep and must be awakened." (1 Kings 18:27).

As the day turned into afternoon, the priests became even more frenzied as still nothing was occurring. They slashed themselves with knives, and spears, drawing blood, as was their practice in their sacrificial offerings in prayer to Baal. They did this until the blood flowed from them. But still there was "no voice; no one answered, no one heeded" (1 Kings 18:20).

Then toward the evening, Elijah had the crowd come in closer to him. Using twelve stones, one to represent each of the tribes of Israel, he rebuilt an old altar that had been left to ruin and had fallen to pieces. Elijah then cut up his bullock and laid the pieces on the firewood and dug a trench around the altar. Then he had some of the bystanders bring buckets of water and instructed them to pour the water out on the altar—drenching the meat and wood and filling the trench.

When this was all ready he called out to God in prayer, "Answer me, O Lord, answer me, that this people may know that thou, O Lord, art God, and that thou hast turned their hearts back" (1 Kings 18:39). This must have been a most incredible sight. At Elijah's call to God fire came down from the sky to the altar that Elijah had constructed. The fire consumed the sacrifice and the wood, and even dried up the water in the trench. The crowd shouted: "The Lord, he is God; the Lord, he is God" (1 Kings 18:39) . . . and they fell on their faces in awe.

Elijah then ordered the priests of Baal to be seized and dragged down to the small Kishon river in the valley below where they were all slain. Then Elijah told Ahab to go home because God was going to send rain to end the drought. Then Elijah went to the top of a ridge and prayed and prayed to God to send rain.

Elijah didn't have an easy time of it. His prayers for rain took patience and time . . . but the rains did come at Elijah's persistence. From then on he was in grave danger. The story continues with more fascinating details, but the main point here is the contest or the ongoing struggle between the forces of good and evil.

The Invisible War

Finally, be strong in the Lord and in his mighty power. Put on the full armor of God so that you can take your stand against the devil's schemes. For our struggle is not against flesh and blood, but against the rulers, against the authorities, against the powers of this dark world and against the spiritual forces of evil in the heavenly realms.

—EPHESIANS 6:10–12

One of my favorite seminary professors, the late Ross Snyder, from whom I learned much at Chicago Theological Seminary, wrote in his book, *inscape*:

Defiance of Difficulties

When it is one more effort or defeat, one more hour or mediocrity,
God of all excellencies, surge in me.
When the going is rough, and men must stand up,
God of the prophets, enter my life,
When the present is a wintry forest; the future, night,
Light which the darkness cannot overcome, be my treasure.
When the unyielding heart of man is adamant, and rallies for his attack wild dragons of exploitive will,
God the transformer, find me with and in you.

I have had my own "praying contests," not only to battle unseen forces without, but to tackle those within. We all do. It is often through difficult times and even through what is called the "darkness of the soul" that we can emerge anew.

And I have been called upon to do battle for others, as well.

Dr. Butterworth has a wonderfully simple way of summing up what prayer is and isn't: Prayer is not something we do to God but to ourselves. It is not a position but a disposition. It is not flattery but a sense of oneness. It is not asking but knowing. It is not words but feeling. It is not will but willingness.

⁓

Know yourself: Within your deepest
discontent . . . lie the seeds of a Solution.

⁓

Americans Speak Out On Prayer

"I pray and pray regularly because I must do it to live."
Father Charles Gonzalez, rector of the Jesuit community at Georgetown University in Washington, D.C.

"I don't look for anything miraculous to happen. The miracle is being able to speak directly to your Maker."
Naji Igram, devout Muslim, Cedar Rapids, Iowa.

"To pray is to bring God back into the world [and] . . . to expand His presence."
The late Rabbi Abraham Joshua Heschel, respected contemporary theologian of the spiritual life.

THE POWER OF PRAYER

*   *   *

The January 6, 1992, issue of *Newsweek* had a fascinating article entitled "Talking to God," which contained a number of very interesting statistics gathered by University of Akron sociologist Margaret Paloma, pollster George Gallup Jr., and the religious research center of sociologist-novelist-priest Andrew Greeley.

Father Greeley's research states that more than 78 percent of all Americans pray at least once a week and more than half (57 percent) pray at least once a day. Indeed, Father Greeley claims that nearly one in five of the 13 percent of Americans who identify themselves as atheists or agnostics still pray daily.

Among the other statistics collected by the three polling groups are the following provocative percentages:

- 91 percent of women pray, as do 85 percent of men.
- 32 percent regularly feel a deep sense of peace when they pray.
- 26 percent regularly sense the strong presence of God.
- 15 percent regularly receive a definite answer to a specific prayer.
- 42 percent ask for material things when they pray.
- Meditative prayer appears to increase with age:

45 percent of the 18–24-year-olds pray meditatively; 70 percent of 65-year-olds do.

- Of those who believe that God exists, 70 percent pray daily.
- 10 percent of those who don't believe in God still pray daily.

In his analysis of the statistics that his research center has amassed, Father Greeley makes the assertion that the frequency of personal prayer is a more reliable barometer of religious commitment than attendance at public worship services.

Rabbi Shira Stern of Monroe township, New Jersey, agrees: "When people come to my temple or a church or a mosque they expect a spiritual experience. But I say that if they haven't done it [prayed] on their own before they step into a sacred place, that place is going to be no more sacred than a library or a movie theater."

The time to pray is not when we are in a
tight spot but just as soon as we get out
of it.—JOSH BILLINGS

In his book *Honest To God*, Bishop John Robinson expresses a sense of frustration where prayer becomes a sacramental ritual "performed by professionals" or "canned prayer" read from a book; "I believe the experts have induced in us a deep inferiority complex. They tell us that this is the way we ought to pray, and yet we find that we cannot maintain ourselves for any length of time even on the lowest rungs of the ladder, let alone climb it. . . . We are evidently not the praying type. And so we carry on with an unacknowledged sense of failure and guilt.

"I can testify to this most strongly from the time I spent in a theological college, both as a student and as a teacher. Here was a laboratory for prayer. Here one ought to be able to pray, if ever one could. If one failed in these circumstances, what hope was there later on—when one was surrounded and sucked down by 'the world'? And yet I believe I am not alone in finding theological college the most difficult rather than the easiest of places in which to pray. In fact, I know I am not. I discovered there what I can only describe as a freemasonry of silent, profoundly discouraged, underground opposition, which felt that all that was said and written about prayer was doubtless unexceptionable but simply did not speak to 'our' condition. But nothing else was offered in its place, and to this day, we have an inferiority complex. We dare not admit to others or to ourselves what non-starters we are."

~

God knows what is in me, I don't need to
tell Him, so I recite prayers to impress a
certain message on myself, my dependence
on God. For I am the addressee: the form
of the prayer is addressed to God, but I am

31

not meant to change God, I'm meant to change myself.—IMMANUEL JAKOBOVITS, CHIEF RABBI

I don't mean to condemn seminary or college guidance and teaching about prayer, but to confess that not only myself, but many of my pastor/priest friends or associates, go by the book. When it comes to "praying to meet special needs," it is at first awkward for many clergy, who at that point would rely on the "established prayers" for all occasions in clerical prayer books.

We should be so comfortable in our conversations with God through prayer that there is no need to feel self-conscious about the words we use and how "theological" the prayer sounds. God is judging our hearts—not our words. This is the secret of prayer fluency—simply pray from the heart.

Fear not, the black holes of Life . . . may give birth to . . . the greatest miracles!

The Way to God . . . Paved With Gold, or a Muddy Road?

Some spiritual disciplines say the only way to know God is to be a renunciate; others say the only way to know God is to have no material possessions, citing that the vow of poverty is the only way one can find true inner spiritual strength. With no objects or duties to perform to keep those objects and to acquire more, they can focus their time on prayer and communion with God.

Others say there is nothing wrong with having things . . . as long as the things don't have you! Still others say that "you can have it all." They tell us that as the children of God, God the Father would want us to have the finest of things. As a matter of fact, others say that we are "the King's kids," therefore, we are heirs to the throne. We should act like princes and princesses and live like kings and queens and truly inherit the Kingdom on Earth.

Then there is the sad truth that there are many who simply don't seem to have a choice . . . they are born into severe poverty, with empty and swollen bellies, bulging eyes, and weakened bones. As cruel as it sounds in one way, there are many who say that this is the way to know God, because it is really only through "suffering" that we can find Him.

So, wherein lies the truth? Is it in one or the other, all of them, or none? In 1968, when I first wrote my book *Seasons of the Soul*, it was apparent to me that somewhere between so many extremes in life was the truth. I wrote:

Somewhere in between summer and winter, happy and sad, good and bad, . . . lies the creative tension of opposites.

All of life is a paradox. There is only a
"charge" in a battery because the negative
and the positive nodes work together in
balance. All of life is "pluses" and
"minuses" . . . cause and effect North Pole
and South Pole . . . summer and winter. The
one extreme cannot exist without the other.
Perfection is found . . . "in the midst of" . . .
in the unity of—the two.

It might be that neither extreme of poverty nor wealth has a "special blessing." There's that old saying, "I've been rich and I've been poor, I like being rich better." Certainly there would seem to be advantages to being rich. I haven't experienced rich in terms of wealth, but I have counseled many who were very wealthy who had lost their joy . . . lost their souls.

At one point in my life, I was stripped of everything and left homeless. I rented a room in a boardinghouse with less than a suitcase of belongings. I worked during the day to pay for room and food. Then I fasted and prayed, attempting to get in touch with what to do to regroup and begin again, and to see if I could find out what was God's plan.

Amazing as it was . . . to have nothing to call my own, it was one of the most valuable lessons of how much we cling to things and think that we cannot do without this or that. It was a very sad time, but I was given a chance to find out who I really was. Oddly, I found a freedom that might never have come to be, without the loss of all that I thought . . . was me.

There was so much less to do as far as dusting and cleaning and washing clothes. No pots or pans or dishes to wash. My needs weren't much, so I didn't have to make very much money to stay in a rooming house. I found I could also eat well without cooking . . . as a matter of fact, I probably haven't eaten as healthy since! I bought just what I needed from day to day, 'cause I didn't have a place . . . to put it away.

⌒

Do not pray for easy lives. Pray to be stronger men. Do not pray for tasks equal to your powers. Pray for powers equal to your tasks. Then the doing of your work shall be no miracle, but *you* shall be the miracle.—PHILLIPS BROOKS

⌒

I made a decision right then and there that I'd spend that whole summer in that simple way. I'd have no ambitions to do anything big . . . not look for embellishment in any single day. I'd stay in one room until I found the real me, I'd add no pressures . . . I would just *be*.

I lost my brother to suicide and my son had just died. There were so many other pains and heartaches inside. It turned out to be a gift . . . to learn what is and what isn't important in life. The things we get so uptight about usually pale . . . to strife.

Nineteen sixty-nine was the summer God spoke to me, because I didn't have things or the pressures blocking my ability "to see."

I have a personal opinion that nothing is bad in and of itself. There is no evil in gold, silver dollars, or dirt. It is not wrong to have a house full of fine furniture and a closet full of clothes. But then it isn't wrong to live in a mud hut and wear just a string. Things aren't good or evil. It is how they are used, how they were gained, how they are maintained. What the attitude *behind* things and *about* things is what matters. For where your treasure is . . . there lies your heart, also.

The same surgeon's hand could:
    beat his wife,
    slap a child
    perform surgery . . . removing a tumor
    feed a baby
    pet his dog
    shake another's hand

But the hand itself . . . is not good or bad. It is the intention and the response of the person who owns that hand. That is true of all life, all things, isn't it? How we react . . . how we use what we have, how we get, how we give. It is our attitude, our heart and soul beliefs, and more importantly . . . *action* . . . *what we think, do or say* that matters—to God.

In the midst of a mystery . . .

Life has set me down in the midst of a mystery.
It seems beyond my fathoming.
Yet I wake and look around me and hear, as it were, a voice saying,
"Seek and you will find. Ask and it will be answered. Knock and it will be opened."
So I seek and I find. But what I find is yet more to seek.
I knock and doors open. But every open door leads to yet another question.
So I see that it is in seeking that I find, and in asking that I am answered.
For the meaning of the mystery—at the point where I can lay hold of it—is contained in the search and the question.
Life has given me a mind to ask and a spirit to seek and hands to knock at its doors.
Yet this much I see clearly—the mystery is not mystery because it is meaningless but because it is meaningful. It is not because things have so little meaning, but because they mean so much that I cannot grasp the meaning . . .

The key called prayer . . .

Life has set me down in the midst of a mystery.
But life has given me a key.

The key is in my own mind.

The key may not take me to the end of the mystery, but it takes me to the beginning.

Having begun, I can go on.

Having taken the first step, I can see to take the next step.

The key life has given me I call prayer.

You may call the key thinking.

Prayer may be thinking.

Thinking may be prayer.

Prayer, to me, is taking thought—but a special kind of thought.

Prayer is a thinking that is more like listening than like speaking.

Prayer is a thinking that sets the mind free. It does not tell the mind what to think; it asks the mind what to think . . .

Prayer is the process of mind by which the unknowable finds meaning and becomes a truth; the unseeable takes shape and becomes a thing of beauty; the immeasurable gains substance and becomes a matter of value.

A way of thought . . .

Prayer then . . . is a way of thought—yet more than a way of thought.

Prayer focuses thought on God the way a compass keeps its needle turned on North.

If I am a traveler, I carry the compass with its needle turning always North, not only when I want to go North, but so that wherever I have to go, I can find the way.

With my thought God-centered, I can go in any direction from that center and not be lost. Though I may not always see my destination, I can find my way.

But it is as true to say of prayer that it is longing as to say that it is thought.

It is as true to say that it is passionate involvement in life.

Prayer is always a reaching beyond ourself toward something greater than ourself.

We may feel that we reach in or out, but always beyond ourself.

Prayer is as much a way of the heart as of the mind and involves the body no less than spirit.

Prayer is the way of the whole man.

I pray when I give the whole of myself to God— or to truth or to beauty or to life or to love or to joy—whatever you prefer to call God or whatever name He may have chosen to reveal Himself by at the moment.

For God Himself is the mystery in which I am set down.

O darkness, are you, then, light—but light so blazing bright that I am blinded by you and must see you only a thought's glow at a time?

Immensity, are you compassion?

Everlasting God, are you my first faint glimmers of truth?

We do not need to know what the sun is in order to see by its light.

It is with God as it is with the sun.

We cannot clasp the vast and flaming orb, but we can live in its warmth a day at a time.

Prayer is my way that I lay hold of Infinite Perfection—a prayer at a time.*

What Should We Ask for in Prayer? Is It Okay to Ask for Things?

Be careful what you ask for because you just might get it! Sometimes what we think would be so right and so perfect for us ends up being big trouble. What is *behind* our asking? What is our motive . . . our attitude? If we should receive something we ask for in prayer and it turns out to be not so good, not to worry, because "All things work out for good for those who love the Lord Thy God." Sometimes there is a valuable lesson that we are to learn and grow from.

⌒

Pray, pray very much; but beware of telling
God what you want.—FRENCH PROVERB

⌒

*Excerpted from: *Prayer: The Master Key*, James Dillet Freeman.

But would we *really* want to pray for something that might not be good for us? Well of course we wouldn't ask . . . if we *knew* that, right? We think we know but we usually don't see the *whole* picture. All teachings on prayer from all the Holy Scriptures seem to agree that to really know what to ask for, it is first essential to know who you are!

In order to know what to ask for in prayer, know *who* you are!

This, of course, doesn't mean your name, address, and social security number! To know *who* we are is to find all of that *within* ourselves, not without. All religions encourage us to look beyond ourselves in order to find the answers within ourselves! More paradox.

The questions that are basic to all spiritual disciplines are:

Who am I?
Why am I here?
What is the meaning of human life?
What is the meaning of right and wrong?
What is the nature of God?
What happens after death?

If the motive or desire is to be One with God, to find the Kingdom of God, to be at peace, and to have harmony and love in your life, then once again, there is a formula to follow.

Perhaps therein is the key of what to ask for. There is a Buddhist story that tells of Gautama meeting up with thirty men while he was on a journey. The men were all running very fast, as if they were all chasing something. Gautama stopped one of them and asked what the trouble was—why were they all in such a hurry?

The man stopped long enough to tell Gautama, panting as he spoke: "We were all having a wonderful time at a picnic when one of our group spotted one of our women companions sneaking away with the belongings of the others. So, we are in pursuit of the thief!"

To that the Buddha responded, "Which do you think is better, to go on chasing this woman, or to go tracking the self?" So the story goes that the Buddha so impacted the men with his answer that they all became followers and disciples of the Buddha. The men decided it would be more fruitful to search for the "real self" rather than running after their belongings.

Gautama said, "I teach only two things, *suffering*, and *release from suffering*." Comparing himself to a doctor who first needed to know how the patient was feeling then tries to diagnose the cause of the illness: "Now this is the Noble Truth as to origin of suffering. It is the craving thirst that causes the renewal of becomings. This craving thirst is accompanied by sensual delights and seeks satisfaction, now here, now there. It takes the form of craving for the gratification of the senses, or the craving for prosperity."

Suffering is the result of a wrong attitude toward the world and our experiences in it. At some point we all either have or have had the craving for popularity, food, success, bigger houses, nicer clothes, faster, newer cars, more money, etc. Consequently, we either have learned or will learn that happiness does not come from things! There might be a kind of fulfillment and a kind of happiness that we experience from these things, but not the kind of happiness that touches the soul and comes from deep within to give us peace of mind. Gautama Buddha's point was that "he who *craves* cannot be free and thus cannot be happy."

Gautama said, "When in following after happiness I have perceived that bad qualities developed and good qualities were diminished, then [there is] that kind of happiness I have perceived that bad qualities were diminished and good qualities developed, then such happiness is to be followed," . . . speaking from his own experience.

~

If God had granted all my silly prayers, where would I be now?—C. S. LEWIS

~

Here is a great parable that comes from the Jewish, Hasidic tradition:

A rabbi saw a man hurrying along the street. He was rushing so fast that he did not look to the left or to the right, just straight ahead. The rabbi managed to catch the man's attention, asking him, "Why are you rushing so much?" The man answered, "I am rushing after my livelihood!" Then the rabbi said, "How do you know that your livelihood is running on before you so that you have to rush after it? Perhaps it is behind you, and all you need is . . . to stand still!"

Jesus, too, said, "It is harder for a rich man to get into heaven than it is for a camel to pass through the eye of a needle." Does this mean that wealth or having nice things is sinful or evil? Does it mean that we should not ask for them in prayer? What all these teachings are saying is *not* that things or money is evil, but it is the *love* of them . . . that is. If the majority of your time is spent in getting and keeping things then there is hardly time left for spiritual development. If you are free to have or not to have . . . then your heart is in the right place, and it is okay to have things.

Can You Live Without it?

Here's another exercise for you to try. Find a comfortable place. Take several long, deep, cleansing breaths. Pray, asking for God to show you if there is something you place higher than Him. Visualize each room in your house. In your mind's eye, walk around the room looking at everything in it. Now, one by one, object by object think of how you would feel if that were taken away. Can you live without it? How does that make you feel? Go on until you have covered your entire home. Don't forget the garage and your cars. Then, what if you were to lose the entire house and everything in it?

Sometimes it is not realistic to just imagine it, but you probably will get enough of a twinge inside, if you strike something that you really would not want to lose. And that's okay! Just a twinge . . . of "Oh, no way, not that!" is not so bad . . . it is normal. But if you really think you'd go nuts then examine that.

I know many families who don't speak to one another because they disagree over who is rightfully entitled to own something after a family member passes away. I even witnessed some of these people beforehand saying they would never let anything like that (referring to other families) happen to them! But they do. As a matter of fact, there are so many whom I know who have bitter, bitter feelings over some teapot or treasure that Aunt Mirdle had that their sister got instead of them. . . . It is very sad to have any thing be more important than a person . . . much less a loved one.

⌒

The fundamental religious point is that in prayer, spiritual energy which otherwise would slumber does become active, and spiritual work of some kind is effected.

⌒

2

How to Pray Effectively

Berkeley Mickelsen, professor of New Testament Greek, says that "people should be taught to pray in God's will." Professor Mickelsen says, "It is the person praying, and not the prayer request or outcome that changes, and that is what makes a prayer effectual."

In *What Happens When Women Pray*, Evelyn Christenson offers some insight into what it means to pray in God's will: "Praying in God's will is not easy, yet it's very simple. It involves a commitment of every single thing that comes into our lives to God and His perfect will. And it's exciting to live in complete oneness with the will of God. It is never dull or static because it is not a one-time, once-for-all commitment. It is something we have to work at constantly, moment by moment."

When Your Prayers Aren't Answered

As president of the United Prayer Ministries, Evelyn Christenson frequently conducts seminars and gives lectures on the subject of prayer. She raises the oft-asked question of what to do when your prayers aren't answered. Re-addressing that the perfect position, as Jesus taught, is to *always* pray in the will of God.

"Praying 'in the will of God' means being conformed to the will of God . . . as we pray." She cites James 5:16. *"Confess your faults, one to another, and pray for one another, that you may be healed. The effectual, fervent prayer of a righteous man availeth much.* The literal translation of "effectual" is: "the effect produced *in the praying person,* bringing him into the will of God."

I also checked the translation for fervent and that you may be healed. Fervent means to turn, or round about or circle. That adds a wonderful dimension to this particular scripture. At first reading, one might think, "oh, I'll go find someone who is very religious and *real* good and ask them to pray for me, or for us . . . (then, I or we will be healed)." So an "effectual person" is more literally one who has been turned around from his/her will to the will of God! (This can take place even as we pray.)

In looking up the original word that would have been translated to mean healing, that, too, has a richer meaning than the translation from one language into another allows with having to choose just one word. "Healing" in this case means "to mount up, to rise up, or to triumph!" Now that could mean that one's physical condition or whatever one is praying for is not healed in the sense that we think of healing. It can also mean a "spiritual triumph" and grace that comes from being in obedience and in accord with God's will—not ours.

In other words, there may be a purpose, a meaning, a lesson for us to learn and grow from in *not* having our requests met, and that very purpose, though it might not be understood, can change your life around!

It's okay to pray for what you think you want for yourself and your loved ones . . . even for the world, but if your prayers aren't answered, it just could be that your angels are looking out for you and the overall Divine Plan overrides your prayer requests. We don't always know best.

———

Reflect . . . someday you will suddenly have
to leave *everything* in this world—so make
the acquaintance of God . . . *now.*

———

So here again, we see that the act of praying is more to affect the pray-er. It is the one who prays who changes. Not God. The prayers allow the pray-er to communicate and come "on-line" with God, if you will! This in itself is life-altering. But as Ms. Christenson says, it isn't easy, but it's simple.

Not too many holy teachers and prophets of old and new, if any, had an easy go of it. Jesus prayed and prayed to God for God to take away the "cup" of what he was about to face. That, of course, was soon to be the crucifixion. In anguish, Jesus continued to beg God, then he added the words "but if it is not possible for this to pass, not my will, but . . . Thy will be done."

The human Jesus did not want to die a torturous death. The spiritual Jesus "turned the human part around" and he accepted that it was not part of the "plan," or the Will of God that his life be spared. He was turned around so completely that while dying on the cross he prayed that God forgive those who crucified him. Now that's compassion.

Sometimes it seems my own life wouldn't be too far from competing with Job with one affliction or hardship after another. Many people I have counseled feel the same is true for them. The overview of the entire world presents a pattern where suffering and inequality, hardship, and strife are often the norm. I believe it is how we respond to what happens to us that makes the difference. This itself might be the reason we are here—to learn to respond to all things hurtful and all people hurtful, with love.

I have mentioned briefly in others of my books that I was blessed to have had Dr. Elisabeth Kübler-Ross as a professor for quite a few courses in seminary. One such course was Church History in Psychoanalytical Perspective. At that time there was big discussion on spiritual suffering as akin to martyrism. I guess it is still an issue with many people. But, in fact, it is through suffering, most often, that the greatest compassion and love emerges.

There were several things that I took issue on with Dr. Ross at the time. She was just teaching her course On Death and Dying and her book of the same title was about to come out. (This was in the '60s.) The things I "took issue" with turned out to be huge issues with both Elisabeth and myself. Over the years, I would think about these with a little anger even. Then one day, it hit me: There were several things that I didn't want to hear because it meant more work for me, but it turned out that she was completely right. This was extremely significant to me because there were few people in my life whom I had that fuming feeling about. I wanted to apologize to her, even though she might not know or remember what the heck I was talking about.

I prayed about it. Time passed. Dr. Ross became very well-known, internationally famous, even. But I was at peace in my heart about the past, having surrendered it entirely to God's will. Then, almost as though a plan had been orchestrated that we reconnect, we did. From that time on we have been extremely close. We turned out to be very significant in each other's life. She had a plan unfold about me, and I had a plan unfold about her.

Life can be so much like that. Amidst so many seemingly random happenings from minute to minute, when one steps back in retreat, in order to examine the past in an overview kind of way, an entire pageant-play emerges (especially if you have surrendered to God's will). It might seem like chaos at the present time, but the integral way that people, places, and things enter our lives—and perhaps exit our lives—can often take on the appearance of a huge jigsaw puzzle that must have been laid out from the start. Then you think, no, it couldn't have been completely laid out, but with each choice or decision you make comes another piece of the puzzle that you might not see how it fits—until a few more are in place. Few of us are wise enough to see that overview. God is. Just look at the order in the Universe (without our human influences, that is)! It is an awesome thing to "really see" the times that one has turned over to God, giving over our will to his, the magic that can unfold!

⌒

"For my thoughts are not your thoughts,
neither are your ways my ways," declares
the Lord. "As the heavens are higher than
the earth, so are my ways higher than
your ways and my thoughts than your
thoughts."—ISAIAH 55:8–9

⌒

To teach us God's ways, there have been prophets, teachers, and spiritual leaders who spent their very lives to do so. Throughout history there have been false prophets, teachers, and spiritual leaders as well, so part of the challenge to humans is to develop the discernment to tell the difference . . . right here on schoolhouse earth!

Be Patient with Prayer

As a counselor, one of the most frequent questions asked of me is: "How can I know what to do with my life?"—and another similar to it is: "How can I find something meaningful to do?"

The answer can come in the most subtle of ways.

Praying about Something Bothering You

For many years I was extremely troubled about those people who were in a situation where even the basics that many of us take for granted were denied to them. I had always prayed for God to bless them or to help them, but it finally dawned on me that the pain and sorrow that I felt on their behalf was gnawing at me at an ever increasing pace. My prayers changed to ask God to show me what I could do about it, if anything.

I learned that the answer to prayer may not come immediately—but not to become discouraged. I believe God will answer a burning desire that you have questions about or are troubled about through subtle glimmers of ideas that come to you out of the blue (or so it might seem!).

One day while I was grocery shopping, my attention was focused on the expiration dates on some of the dairy products. A carton of milk that I had in hand happened to have an expired date on it, so I asked the manager what he did with items such as that. When he told me that they might sell it for half price on that date but after that date they were to dispose of them by law, I was dismayed.

First I bought quite a few items for half price and noticed that there was nothing wrong with the taste. Milk wasn't sour, yogurt was as good as ever, and even sour cream, whipping cream, etc., tasted fine. I experimented with freezing items and discovered they might change slightly in consistency when thawed out, but the dairy products especially were great to use in casserole dishes or in baking.

Wallowing in the sands of your sorrows . . .
    makes only quicksand—to sink in despair.

The old idea lightbulb went off in my head. I checked into day-old bread and rolls, dented cans, boxes that were slightly squashed, and found that all these items were also not saleable items. The waste of so much food, most of which was perfectly fine, in this one store alone completely shocked me.

People all around this area were going hungry, yet this store was throwing away food! No telling how many other stores in the area there were that no doubt did the same, I thought. Suddenly it made an impact on me that *this* was at least one answer to my prayers. Instead of questioning God about the unfairness of so many poor and suffering people, as I had for so long, changing *my* attitude and asking in prayer to turn my despair into some way I could help provided an avenue for God to answer me.

There is no doubt in my mind that it was almost as though an angel had appeared on the scene to open my eyes to a direct way I could make a difference. I could have just bought a few half-priced items for myself and been happy at my discovery of a new way to save money. I also could have been inspired by the idea I had of coordinating pickups and delivery of the food, but leaving it for someone else to do. After all, I was already too busy with classes and work.

I believe that if the emotion and intensity of your prayers are genuine, and you let the receptivity within you remain open and patient for an answer, it will come. I asked, and here He was showing me— by drawing my attention to the immense waste. However, it was up to me to pay attention.

I started by asking the manager what the procedure would be if I coordinated the out-of-date, day-old, dented cans and all else that would be food for those in need. That was the beginning of many massive efforts that I coordinated for pickups and distribution of food for those in need. This was in the mid-sixties, when nothing to my knowledge was being done along this line, so my questions were not met with immediate answers, but I was pleasantly surprised by the willingness and cooperation of the manager finding out.

Without getting into the particulars, this was the birth of many years of my doing this kind of thing on the side and attempting to set up situations wherever I went, where a permanent type of plan was set into motion for others to coordinate for the various communities. I found the same to be true for toys for children at Christmas time and clothes for the needy, supplies for the schools and churches, and a limitless range of "throw-aways" converted to blessings for many—and *an answer to prayer!*

Often we think there is magic in a certain prayer formula, an amulet or a ritual. There is a great story I've heard from an old Hassidic tradition. The story is referred to as the Sacred Prayer:

Whenever misfortune threatened the village, the rabbi would retreat to a special place in the forest, light a sacred fire, and say a special prayer. The misfortune was then avoided. As time passed, this task fell to another rabbi who knew the special place in the forest and the special prayer, but he did not know how to light the sacred fire. Still misfortune was avoided. Eventually it fell to a third who knew the place in the forest but did not know how to build the sacred fire or recite the special prayer. Even this, though, was enough to avert the misfortune. Finally the task fell to yet another rabbi over the years who knew neither the place in the forest, how to light the sacred fire nor even the special prayer. All he could do was tell the story of the others. But that was sufficient!

Every Thought Is a Prayer

"All our thoughts, all our conscious thinking, is in essence part of a prayer." Ambrose Worall encouraged people to think about prayer in this new way, a way "that is usually not considered to be prayer." To elaborate, Worall said, "For as a man thinketh, so he is. Indeed, as he thinketh, so he prays. Millions of people, in many varieties of religions, pray—without thought, without purpose, reciting empty words that no longer have meaning to the one mouthing them because he does not listen to them himself, with his mind or heart or soul; he mumbles them with vague meaningless mumblings.

> True prayer is nothing but love.
> —St. Augustine

When I first heard Ambrose talk about this belief, it struck a chord within me and my own beliefs. This was what I interpreted the teachings of Jesus to mean, *to live each moment as if it were a prayer*. One of my favorite sayings from the '60s and '70s was one that I made into a plaque to hang on the wall to remind me:

God gave you the gift of *life*.
Your gift to God is *how you live* that life!

To me that means that God gave us the miracle of life beginning anew every second. We could totally change our life around ten seconds from now—if we choose to! In essence, our very lives are the compilation of many seconds. Each one of those seconds we had, have, or still have a new chance to begin again. It all starts with each and every thought we think.

Begin Again

Here are a couple of techniques that I developed for myself and for those I have counseled, to begin to monitor your thoughts about yourself. These are the first steps to living your life as a prayer:

1. If you don't like who you are, stop and evaluate your own thoughts about who you think you are.

    This might sound simple, but do this over a week or so, and you'll begin to see the complexity of mixed thoughts. Keep a journal. Make time for prayer for whatever time you realistically know you will be able to keep. Maybe start with just five minutes in the morning and five minutes at night.

2. Immediately after your prayers, spend about the same amount of time in meditation/contemplation. Just sit and *notice* your thoughts.

Technique Before Prayer

1. Choose a time when you will have the least interruptions. My personal preference is to start the day and end the day with conscious prayer. Before your feet even touch the floor in the morning is a good time to take whatever time you have decided on for prayer. Or, to be certain you don't fall right back to sleep, maybe get up and splash cold water on your face, brush your teeth, etc., then go back and sit, lie, or whatever is most, but not too, comfortable.

2. Take several very deep, long, and slow breaths, exhaling all air each time slowly. To prime the pump, sometimes, if not all the time, say a prayer you know such as the Lord's Prayer silently, or out loud, it doesn't matter. Then focus on calling on God in whatever personal way you choose, even if it is only as simple as "God, be with me today, help me pray for anyone who

comes to mind, or for any thing (such as victims of the hurricane you saw on the news).

3. For the meditation time, do the same with relaxing techniques, and deep cleansing breaths. Then try *not* to think . . . but to *listen*. Most likely the first thoughts will be I've got to get going, I don't have time to sit here! Whatever else pops in notice it. If it is a negative thought, just develop a technique that works for you in order to deal with it. Visualize yourself throwing the thought away into a garbage can, or simply say something (in your mind) like "be gone" or "out."

Don't beat yourself up if all the thoughts are negative. Training your mind is no different from taming an extremely wild horse; you just need consistency and patience. When your subconscious gets the message on your consistent prayer/meditation time, it will begin to cooperate more with you. Soon either ideas, inspiration, or answers to prayer will start to come. You will know when they are right.

At first you might want to set a timer, if you are in need of leaving for work or class, etc. Even if you fall asleep during the time allotted, don't give up. I have done that more times than I could count. That is real normal, as that is what your body is used to doing. If you are either sitting or lying down, and there is no TV on, no book, no conversation, your body remembers "oh, none of the normal things are going on, it must be time to go to sleep again." Just keep on keeping on without feeling guilty that the prayer meditation time doesn't seem lucrative. It, like everything else, takes time and practice. Practice is something we are not used to thinking of in the context of prayer . . . at all!

Write down your thoughts during prayer and what came to your mind to pray for. Then do the same for meditation. Write down the random thoughts that you noticed—no matter how silly or insignificant they might be. This is "for your eyes only." You can consider this a Top Secret project to find out more about the person known as you!

Throughout the day and evening, try to be aware of your every thought. Train yourself to evaluate your thoughts as one of only two possibilities: one, *positive;* two, *negative.* Try to remember to write down a "tally" at least several times (in your notebook). For instance, by about noon, if you were to add up all of your thoughts, would they be mostly positive, mostly negative, or about equal, or all positive or all negative? Be honest. You have nothing at all to gain by "fudging." The point is for you to get in touch with how often thoughts go unnoticed. These add up. In general you might think that you are really a positive-thinking person, maybe an optimist even!

Religion's in the heart, not in the knee.
—DOUGLAS JERROLD

Most of us have to literally train ourselves to watch our negative thoughts and retrain them into positive. By the very process of growing up and fitting in we have adopted all kinds of thoughts we think—habitually. The same, of course, is true for what we say. What comes out of our mouth was first in our heads as thoughts! Most often we completely think, say, and do as a routine, until we Stop, Notice, Redirect.

Do this for at least a month if possible. At the end of even one day, your attention should become more and more focused to what really goes on inside that head! None of us is exempt from negative thoughts. Not even saints. Study the life of any saint. There is always the battle of positive and negative thoughts. A saint is just a sinner who never gave up!

Now, the real trick will come when you also begin to notice how many people around you are negative. To not respond *to* negativity *with* negativity is the challenge. If someone says something unkind or a bit nasty to you, bite your tongue if you have to. If something negative "just slips out," out of habit, at least you will *notice* it. If possible try to add these to your journal.

Negative Thought Is Negative Prayer

Each thought that you think sets up a vibration all its own. You are the composite of not only all the events that happened from birth on, living within a body of bones and flesh, but you are the composite of all the thoughts that you think about what has happened and is happening and will happen. That last part puts *you* in the driver's seat. You may have had a lot of real bad things happen to you, like me, like many others; but the prayerful difference is our *response* to the happenings!

The way of the world or the world's typical response to negative thoughts, things, places, events, people is:

- fight or flight
- hit back
- don't let them do that to you
- don't let them say that to you
- they (he, she) won't get away with this
- strike first, make the first punch (whether physical or verbal), so you are one-up
- I'll show them (or him or her), just wait!
- get even

We don't come with a manual at birth for our parents to learn how to treat us every minute with love. We carry on the negative patterns we learned growing up, as well as the positive. But there is no need to wait until we have no idea "who" we are and what our own separate identity is from that of our parents or our environment.

If we respond to any negative thing *with* negativity, then we are just as bad as the who or what behind the negative. Make sense? All the sacred teachings of all religions boil down to that! Learn, train yourself to stop with the negative prayer, which is each and every moment we have negative thoughts, to think and pray positive. *Make your every thought positive.* I promise you that if you can master this, you will become a master. But then again, it probably will take your whole life of learning and trying.

As I wrote in *Seasons Of The Soul*, the word *sin* comes from a Hebrew word meaning "muddy" or "off the mark." The word *repent* means to "change your mind or direction." These are two words that have more judgment with them and are so misused among words! Think about the original meaning of sin, which hasn't changed, but maybe the *connotation should* change. If we sin, we have missed the mark (being a bull's-eye or dead center).

REPENT!

Here's another technique to try:

Picture your life as a giant dartboard. Add this to your journal. (Draw a dartboard using many, many rings around the center bull's-eye. We will not stick to a regulation dartboard outline—this is real life.) Think of major events in your life and your response to them. Make a symbolic mark where each of those events fall on the dartboard. If you reacted "really bad," you're off the chart, missed it entirely. If you could have done better, but were kind of on-target, you might be in the circle ring outside the bull's-eye.

Now, the repent part. Your gift today is that you can start *now with the power of prayer to ask for God's help to help you "re-aim" every single thought—to the bull's-eye. The bull's-eye is perfect love. The bull's-eye is God.*

With every breath you *take* . . you are *given* the change to *begin again!*

Don't be discouraged if it seems like an overwhelming task. At first you will think, "no problem, how could this be hard?" but it is. Monks of old used to beat themselves with whips for each negative thought. There are still some different spiritual groups around the world that either cut themselves, whip themselves, or do some severe physical abuse to themselves—each time they "miss the mark." There is certainly no need to do that, but I am telling you that the discipline takes a lifetime and is the best investment for your future you will ever make! The only thing that can happen is that you will continue to get better and better.

The Nail-Polish Sin

I'll never forget when I was in London on business. It was approximately 1980 and what a mix of people everywhere. It was fascinating. As I was walking down one of the main streets, a kindly looking old man caught my attention as he handed me something to read. It turned out to be a religious tract saying "Do you know Jesus?" I glanced at that, then quickly responded by smiling and saying yes, I do, have a blessed day, when he seized my hand, turning it over so that my palm with the tract still in it was facing down toward the street. His face turned from kindly to a scowl and his voice from loving to a shrill judgment cry of: "No, you don't know Jesus, you Jezebel, no you don't know Jesus. . . . Look at this!" At that he "threw" my hand down in disgust like I had poison ivy or something. Confused at the sudden Dr. Jekyll and Mr. Hyde act that took place in record time, I said, "What, what are you talking about?" Without missing a beat, he said, "Nail polish. You have nail polish on, you sinner, you Jezebel!"

Well, I needn't tell you that wearing nail polish wasn't in the Ten Commandments (not to my knowledge anyway). Maybe it is in this man's holy book, but none that I have ever seen! The funny thing is that I almost *never* wore nail polish! I never took the time to do my nails. I was always too busy for polish to stay on anyway! But for this meeting I was going to, I decided, what the heck, I had a little time in my room to do my nails!

The point is that "sinner," or this is a sin or that is a sin has many connotations and the misunderstanding of which has pulled more people away from the church probably than brought them to it. How ridiculous that he thought I was a sinner because I had pink nail polish on. Lord only knows what he told some of the purple-and-orange hair people with black nail polish and rhinestones on!

I was raised in my Grandma and Papa Johnson's home until I was eight or nine years old. They were the most loving people you'd ever want to meet, both from Sweden. Everything seemed to be a sin! We went to the United Brethren Church where Papa was the Caretaker and bell ringer. I helped dust the pews and run the floor polisher (when I could beg Papa to let me try for three minutes!). Here is where our family learned that card playing, game playing, dancing, movies, etc., etc., were all—a sin!

Many of us were raised that way, to a point anyway. I still might feel guilty about the nail polish, because I still hardly ever wear it. But the main point is that we can be so silly about what is missing the mark, or sin, and what isn't. There are definitely things that we would be better off for not involving ourselves in, but they might not be a sin. Like nail polish. When we study the Commandments and what Jesus said, that the Commandments all could be distilled down to the first two . . . Love God with all your heart, mind, and soul (no other gods) and love and treat others as you wish to be treated. That's it. Basically, that is what is a real sin. We miss the mark every time we don't do these two.

Sorting It Out

Continue writing in your journal your thoughts during prayer and meditation time. If you have done the "bull's-eye" chart, notice there what you have recorded as "missing the mark" or a sin. When you evaluate each thing, was the missing the mark or the sin something that you were taught was a sin like nail polish or really missing the mark for hurting someone with a word, act, or deed, or worse? If you have not done so already in your life, ask God to forgive you, then forgive yourself and *re-aim*. Think and pray about the kind of person you want to be and the responses you wish and pray to have. God gives us a new gift with every next minute of life we have—to repent, to change, to be better.

Notice people's response to you after the first month or so that you have been sticking to the technique of making yourself aware of your thoughts and words. Has anyone said to you, "There's been something different about you . . . you are much kinder"? Maybe people will start treating you better, maybe not. We aren't to do this for the response but just notice.

⌒

Human conduct is ever unreliable . . . until
man is anchored in the Divine.

Everything in future will improve . . . if
you are making a spiritual effort now.

⌒

Then notice the pressure placed on you by your peers. Do you treat people differently because it is cool to only be in with a certain crowd and uncool to be nice with the uncool? My family moved around a whole lot from the time I was nine years old. I went to sixteen schools before college. Every time we moved and I was the "new kid." It seemed like the rules were all the same no matter what part of the country my school was in.

As an example, I was in the library at Grosse Pointe High School, in Grosse Pointe, Michigan. We had just moved there and this was my first week at school. Several girls had asked me for help on a topic in the library. I helped this one girl look something up and quietly we talked (just a little, since you aren't supposed to talk in library, right?). When the bell rang, three girls came rushing up to me, and said, "Hey, just a word of advice . . . if you want to be popular, there are some people you just *don't talk to,* don't even smile at them." Then they proceeded to tell me why.

It is amazing how many adults do something similar. It even happens in church. So many families and kids I have counseled have shared secret hurts if they were not in the "in crowd." Jesus was in trouble with his own disciples for the same thing. How upset they were that he would dare eat in a home of a "dreaded tax collector," or let a prostitute pour oil on his feet, washing them with her hair. Nobody is the "out crowd" when you are living in the Spirit, or in the

Will of God. That doesn't mean that you hang out, it means you treat all people with kindness and love.

Yogis, Native-American shamen, mentalists, karate masters (and other martial arts), musicians, dancers, Olympic medalists—they all have mastered part of their thoughts aimed at what they want to accomplish. The biggest-kept secret of this must be "why don't we *all want* to master our thoughts to become loving and good people?"

~ 3 ~

What's the Difference Between Prayer and Positive Thinking?

The difference is calling on God's' Power (the Holy Spirit) to help. Without God's help, the way of the world is too strong when it comes to us turning the other cheek or being kind to those who are mean to us. It is being loving *in spite of* conditions around us that push us to be negative.

It is tough enough with the power of thought or concentration to become a yogi, or a medal-winning Olympist, or to master anything; but it is much, much, much tougher when it comes to *emotional, mental, and physical responses to how we are treated*. It must be the most difficult thing in all of life to accomplish. Look at how few have throughout the history of the planet! That's what it will take for families to be the loving support base. That's what it will take for peace and harmony in everything.

Help us, this and every day,
To live more nearly as we pray—JOHN KEBLE

That's what religion is all about. Jesus said, "Pray for those that persecute you," "Do good to those who spite you," "Be kind to those that hurt you." "Love your enemy" doesn't necessarily mean go give him a hug but it *does* mean don't be mean back. I wonder if Jesus knew that as much as he was teaching these "foreign and alien concepts" that he would give the best example while he was being nailed to the cross. With love in his heart, he looked right at those who had whipped, scourged, and put the crown of thorns on his head, and who had now finished pounding nails through his wrists and feet, attaching him to his death cross, and he still said, "Eli (Father) . . . forgive them, they don't know what they are doing."

Certainly Jesus knew—they knew—what they had done and were doing physically. What Jesus was referring to was their "spiritual and mental knowing," that they *did not know*. That, I believe, each one of us, no matter who we are, no matter what our background, religion, race, color, or creed has to do—*know ourselves*.

Scriptures tell us that. This means every single thought. That is the goal, then we can move from being merely human to bringing the help of God in, the *spirit* of God into us to become spiritual or super-human. A laser light has power only because each electron is marching in the very exact same direction. In normal light, the electrons are all random and scattered. It is through "lasering our thoughts to God" that we gain true spiritual power.

Jesus said: You are the temple of God
              You are the light of the world
              You are the salt of the earth

We must look within. It is there we find the power to make every thought a prayer. The more your thoughts start going in the *same direction*, the more power your thoughts will have and the more power your prayers will have! Think about it. Then, pray about it!

Prayerful Thinking

Again, Ambrose Worrall said, "In mere thought-*lessness* there can be no prayer." He said in *The Healing Gifts of the Spirit*, a book by him and his wife, Olga, "Whether or not we go to church regularly, we still lead prayerful lives, though we may not know it. If we wish a man sick, it is a prayer, but a prayer for sickness, not good. If we think ill of him, it is a prayer, again of evil. If, in our mind, we see him in failure, it is a prayer for his failure. If we see him healthy, successful, if we think of him in terms of love, if we surround him and his family in our thoughts with love—this is prayer. Whatever we think about others, about ourselves, our world, becomes a prayer for or against others, for or against ourselves, for or against our world."

⌒

Worship is an *ongoing* action. The act of
prayer is from *moment to moment*.

⌒

Negative Prayer and Healing
"Prayer is *not* like turning on the oven"

Dr. Daniel J. Benor, M.D., in his *Healing Research, Volume I*, says: "Prayer is not like turning on an oven." What does he mean? "We ask in prayer because we are not in control. Maybe we want a quick fix—we want God to solve our problem, when we need to be doing the work ourselves.

"The reason for illness may be beyond our immediate comprehension. We may have lessons to learn through illness or other problems. Part of our lesson may be with people who are close to us. Maybe we have not learned to ask for help from those around us. Part of healing may be releasing old hurts.

"Some cancer patients believe that they allowed cancer to develop because their life situations, either personal or professional, were intolerable. They didn't see a way out. It can take a long time to get those awarenesses behind the illness."

One of my favorite illustrations as an example of using prayer for the means to an end, one's *own* end, comes from Mark Twain. A misunderstanding of Miss Wilson's attempt to explain about prayer to little Huck in *Huckleberry Finn*:

> Miss Wilson she took me in the closet and prayed, but nothing come of it. She told me to pray every-day and whatever I asked I would get it. But it warn't so. I tried it. Once I got a fish line, but no hooks. I tried for the hooks three or four times, but somehow I couldn't make it work. By and by, one day, I asked Miss Wilson to try for me, but she said I was a fool. She never told me why, and I couldn't make it out no way.

You Can't Always Get What You Want?

Mick Jagger echoed the plaint of millions when he sang that we cannot always get what we want.

There are many scriptures that if taken literally, tell us that we *can* have anything we want if we simply ask and believe.

~

And all things, whatsoever ye shall ask in prayer, *believing*, ye shall receive.
—MATTHEW 21:22

~

This is one of the most powerful promises given to

us by Jesus. Does this mean *literally* that we can pray for anything that we want—and receive it? Although myriad people who read the scriptures may interpret some of the quotations literally, when they are closely examined, a slightly different meaning seems couched within the teachings.

Just before making this statement to his disciples, Jesus had given them an illustration. They had journeyed to Bethany for the night's rest, and in returning to Jerusalem, Jesus was hungry.

He saw a fig tree apparently abundantly full with leaves that we can guess must have looked like a welcome source of food to the hungry Jesus and his followers. When they got closer to the tree, Jesus saw *only* the leaves—no fruit at all—no figs. If you have ever had the pleasure of picking figs fresh from a tree, you would know that the leaves shelter and protect the figs, sometimes making it difficult to see them until you actually lift and separate the leaves to reveal the fruit. So it is understandable that they would think the tree to be a plentiful and timely source of nourishment—from a distance.

Finding no fruit, Jesus did a surprising thing: he *cursed* the fig three with an admonishment for all time. From that day forward, he issued a proclamation that it would *never* bear fruit again. The disciples, no doubt, must have been somewhat stunned by Jesus' action.

Certainly, they would not have been surprised to see the demonstration of power that their teacher had displayed. By now they would have witnessed miracle after miracle. But according to the accounts in the New Testament, all of the supernatural things they witnessed Jesus doing were in the nature of healing or helping—not cursing! They probably had never seen Jesus curse or harm anything.

The Gospels tell us the disciples were "marveling over" how fast the fig tree responded to their Master's words by withering away right before their eyes! That's when Jesus responded to their amazement by telling them that *they* were capable of doing just such a thing. Actually, he told them they could even take on something much larger than a fig tree— a whole mountain!

Jesus told them that if they had faith and did not doubt, not only would they be able to do the same exact thing, but they would also be able to make a whole mountain move by simply commanding it to do so. Was Jesus telling them that they would be able to have power over nature?

I wonder how many times this scene has been dramatized in church plays with humor: "Come on now, Jesus, that is a *big* mountain! Couldn't we start with an ant hill or something smaller?" Not to be sacrilegious at all here, but how many of us have wondered all of our lives if that is supposed to be literal! The rest of what Jesus said was that the disciples could even command the mountain to slide into the sea—and it would.

Then Jesus gave the *promise*. "And ALL things,

whatsoever ye ask in *prayer, believing, ye shall receive."* Here the word believing is sometimes translated as "faith" or vice versa. But for all practical purposes, they mean the same thing. Either word holds one of the keys to understanding the promise, which we will come back to.

First, do you really think that this promise means we can ask God in prayer for *anything at all?* My car is about seven or eight years old, how about a new Jaguar or even a Rolls-Royce? I might as well ask for the top of the line if nothing is impossible. What about moving on up to that beautiful home in the mountains or on the ocean, we are desperate for more space.

~

> We should spend as much time in thanking
> God for His benefits as we do in asking
> him for them.—ST. VINCENT DE PAUL

~

Many are preaching and teaching these days that nothing is too good for you in the eyes of God, and that it is the Father's good pleasure to give you *whatever you want!* I believed it was true with all my heart, until I had a life-altering experience that changed my own understanding of this teaching. (Later in the book, I will share with you what that was.) Although I did not personally believe that it was right to "trouble God" with material requests, and did not do so, when we really think about it if it were really that easy, wouldn't we all be living in great abundance and prosperity if most of us asked for it? The thing is, we *are*—it is just a very different kind of abundance and prosperity.

This is *not* to say that there is anything wrong with the finest of things. Wealth and prosperity are not evil. It is all that goes with the wealth or bigger and better goods that is the problem. If that is where our focus of attention is, therein is the problem. "Where your treasure is, there is your heart also." Jesus also said, "You can't serve two masters and do either of them justice" (referring to money and God). Next is when Jesus said, "It is harder for a rich man to enter the Kingdom of Heaven than it is for a camel to go through the eye of a needle." (This we mentioned earlier.)

Like a great many other things, the Bible seems to contradict itself in many teachings. At first appearance, it is confusing, that is why the Bible can't just be read, but it needs to be *studied* in order to understand the full context. So, what is Jesus telling us here? Do you think that it is possible to have anything at all we want?

For one thing, if we were to receive fulfillment from every single prayer request we made to God, it would make God more like a fairy-tale genie in a magic Aladdin's lamp—only with unlimited wishes and instead of rubbing a lamp, we would pray.

God is much much more than a genie in a magic lamp. But perhaps there is still an adolescent within us all at times that wants what we want, when we want it, and that is usually *now*! Or at the very least *soon*!

⁓

> God is not a cosmic bell-boy for whom we
> can press a button to get things.—HARRY
> EMERSON FOSDICK, *The Meaning of Prayer*

⁓

Dr. Venice Bloodworth affirms in his book, *Keys to Yourself,* that ever since the dawn of human existence and through all the succeeding ages humankind has recognized the mighty invisible force that governs and controls the universe.

As we look around at the order and endless beauty of nature and the heavens, deep within every one of us there must be that sense of awestruck amazement and in our heart and our very gut we must know that "God, Allah, The Great Spirit, The Great Mystery, or whichever the over 100 names there are for *God . . . knows best!*"

To illustrate, there is a wonderful story I heard told by Dr. Robert H. Schuller. Dr. Schuller is the "possibility thinker" with the wonderful inspiring *Hour of Power* television ministry that airs most places on Sundays. He told of a legend he heard that came from Germany:

> Years ago, we were troubled with poor harvests. So the villagers prayed, "Lord, for one year promise us that you will give us exactly what we ask for—sun and rain, when we ask for it."

According to the legend, God agreed. When the villagers called for rain, He sent rain. When they called for sun, He sent sun. Never did the corn grow taller, or the wheat so thick as it did that season.

As the harvest time approached, joy turned to sadness when the farmers in the village saw to their shock and dismay that the cornstalks, although tall, had no corn. The wheat stalks, in spite of being thick, produced no grain. And the abundant leafy fruit trees bore no fruit.

"Oh Dear God!" the simple people prayed. "You have failed us."

And God replied, "Not so my children. I gave you all that you asked for."

"Then why—why, Lord," they cried. "Why is it that we have no fruit or kernel or grain?"

"Because," God answered, "you did not ask for the harsh north wind. In avoiding the winds, there is no pollination."

The human part of us is apt to forget one of *the most* essential things—if we were in charge! God gave us free will, but it really is wonderful that none of us is in full command of the universe and beyond! We should gladly relinquish the controls to Him/Her God, and say with conviction, "God, only You know better than I what my needs are, may Thy will be done!"

Haven't you at one time or another felt totally convinced that there was something or someone so right for you that you could barely "live" if you didn't get it, only to find out later that your insight wasn't so keen after all; in fact, it was completely off kilter! I know I have—*many times*!

If God were to grant each and every person every single prayer request, for one thing, there would be total chaos. To expect God to answer all prayer requests means we would have constant miracles. What could be wrong with that? What then of all the hate, bad feelings, and desires to harm, punish, or get rid of one's enemy? It would be "heaven" if none of the bad thoughts and deeds were present within all God's creatures; but we merely have to look around to see as they say, "that ain't so"!

In the article "The Message of Miracles," in the April 10, 1996, issue of *Time* magazine, Nancy Gibbs says that an angry Jesus asked, "Why does this generation ask for a sign?"

She says he might as well be asking the same question today of our generation. "Touch me, heal me, the crowds demanded of their Messiah, and so even as he went about touching and healing, it was as if he acknowledged that miracles, if produced on demand, *could sabotage the faith they were meant to strengthen.*" Jesus didn't heal *all* people in need. There were too many of them, and perhaps *not all* were to be healed.

It is probably an accurate observation to say that "for the truly faithful, no miracle is necessary; for those who must doubt, no miracle is sufficient."

I think our deep inner self must know on some level that we are here on "schoolhouse earth" to grow, to learn, to love. Somehow we became more fascinated by the "toys" and forgot the real essence and meaning of life, of our *purpose*.

In Luke 12:15, Jesus says, "Watch out! Be on your guard against all kinds of greed; a man's life does not consist in the abundance of his possessions." So, as with everything in life, we need to examine not just the things Jesus said that we like, but all of what he said, that we may have the whole picture.

While it is true that Jesus *did* say, not only once, but *many* times that the miracles he did could be done by us, if we ask in prayer, we can see there must be more to the meaning than to grant magic wishes. Sadly, this has caused many to stumble and feel God isn't really there and doesn't care—because their prayers weren't answered.

The answer to Jesus' own prayers to God for the miracles he demonstrated were asked and given out of deep compassion for our suffering and out of a mission to teach us the way to turn ourselves around and to live life in a more fulfilling way that was meant for us, by demonstrating for us what is possible. Even for the Master, not all His prayers were answered! Nor was he spared from great suffering and pain, yet he *always* surrendered to God's will.

Just suppose for one moment, if you were God would you trust humankind's ability to discern the real needs from their selfish desires? Looking around once more at the state of human affairs and pollution, destruction to the environment, abusing, competing, and killing one another in killing fields across the globe it would appear obvious that in spite of millions of good, kind, and loving people, the majority are caught up in greed.

>

"Does God always answer prayer?" the cardinal was asked. "Yes," he said, "and sometimes the answer is no."
—ALISTAIR COOKE, BBC RADIO

>

I said that I would come back to the command for a mountain to move and to slide into the sea. The well-known theologian Rocco Errico has a doctorate in Theology. He tells us that Jesus most likely spoke Aramaic, not Greek as seminarians learn, or perhaps he spoke both. But in relating to the people, he would have spoken in their native language. Dr. Errico says that commanding the mountain to be uprooted and fall into the sea is an Aramaic idiom. "It refers to the ability to conquer any obstacle, regardless of the difficulty involved."

In his book, *Gospel Light*, Dr. G.M. Lamsa tells us that nowhere is there any record about the disciples literally uprooting mountains. Dr. Lamsa says that extravagant expressions are common in Aramaic and Hebrew speech. He says that these exaggerations of speech never cause misunderstanding because people know the speaker does not mean exactly what he says.

Jesus, then, was encouraging his disciples with

their soon-to-be status as healers of spiritual, mental, and physical ailments of people who were "not curable" by the world's standards. He was enhancing the point that they were not simply "ordinary men" but they were endowed with supernatural abilities through their spiritual powers as Jesus was demonstrating.

Who rises from his prayer a better man, his prayer is answered.—GEORGE MEREDITH

The following is one of my favorite prayers. I've seen it attributed to St. Francis, but usually it is simply listed as source "unknown."

I Asked God

I asked God for strength,
    that I might achieve.
I was made weak,
    that I might learn to obey.

I asked God for health,
    that I might do great things.
I was given infirmity,
    that I might do better things.

I asked God for riches,
    that I might be happy.

I was given poverty,
   that I might be wise.

I asked God for power,
   that I might have approval.
I was given weakness,
   that I might feel the need for God.

I asked for all things,
   that I might enjoy life.
I was given life,
   that I might enjoy all things.

I got nothing that I asked for,
   but everything I hoped for,
I am among all people,
   most richly blessed!

—St. Francis

His safest haven was prayer; not of a single
   moment or idle, but prayer of long
devotion . . . walking, sitting, eating or
drinking, he was always intent upon prayer.
   —THOMAS OF CELANO, *Life of St. Francis*

4

The Place of Prayer in Our Lives

Some men will spin out a long prayer telling
God who and what He is, or they pray
out a whole system of divinity. Some people
preach, others exhort the people, till
everybody wishes they would stop and God
wishes so, too, most undoubtedly.
—CHARLES FINNEY,
Lectures on Revivals of Religion

Author, screenwriter, playwright, novelist, Harold
Sherman has been a "spiritual hero" of my husband
Brad's since the early 1950s. But it wasn't until 1970
that the two men met each other in person. They
immediately established an instant rapport.

Brad was recently remembering his eagerness upon finally meeting Harold Sherman: "I was talking so excitedly and rapidly about my admiration for him and his accomplishments, rattling off many of them that I was familiar with, when Sherman started to laugh. He turned to his wife, still laughing, and said, 'Martha, this man knows more about me than I do!' "

Their friendship led to numerous dual appearances on lecture platforms throughout the United States and many delightful and insightful conversations that went on for hours at a time. In addition, they corresponded regularly and spoke often over the telephone.

Sherman had received international attention in 1937 when the Russian aviator Sigismund Levanevsky and his five-man crew vanished while on a daring flight over the polar regions. The Soviet government prevailed upon the famous British Arctic explorer Sir Hubert Wilkins to conduct a search for the missing airmen.

Just before Sir Hubert left on his mission, he had lunch with Harold Sherman. Harold was known for having an uncanny ability to "tune in on things." Some call it "word of knowledge," others call it a spiritual sensitivity, still others call it psychic ability. (The word psychic comes from psyche, which means soul.) The two men discussed the case and they agreed to attempt to remain in telepathic contact with each other as a kind of experiment.

For purposes of this book, it is not necessary to go into detail, but suffice it to say Harold Sherman picked up on extraordinary details about the progress of Sir Hubert's expedition, which were surprisingly accurate. He had been able to determine the location of the expedition, the events that Sir Hubert observed, and the mechanical difficulties that the explorer was having with the plane that he flew.

Reginald Iverson, who had been hired by the *New York Times* to keep in radio contact with Sir Hubert's search party, found that sunspot and magnetic conditions had made regular communication impossible, and he had been able to get through to Sir Hubert on only a very few occasions. In an affidavit, which Iverson signed after the unsuccessful search for the Russian aviators had been completed, he testified that Harold Sherman had been able to receive more accurate knowledge via telepathy with Sir Hubert than he had been able to gain from his sporadic radio contact with the expedition.

Brad knew Harold as a wise, gentle, extremely devout man, who always spoke in a down-to-earth, straightforward manner about spiritual matters. For the rest of his long and fruitful life, Harold Sherman worked tirelessly to devote his spiritual energies toward helping ordinary men and women.

Harold always said that prayer, rightly understood and exercised, can lead every sincere seeker to a more direct and knowing communication with God.

However, the act of prayer, he firmly believed, is

distinctly an individual proposition. Each of us must find God in his or her own way.

Harold was impatient with mere lip service being given to God in high places and with "hollow utterances of praises and thanksgiving." And he was critical of religious groups that sought so hard to be "influential, right, and conventional" that they emphasized form rather than spirit in their many prayers.

"The only Source that you ever need to reach and impress is the God Presence within you," he said. "When this relationship is knowingly established on a day-to-day basis, you will be the recipient of new inspiration, guidance, and protection far beyond your ordinary human capacity. But you must be willing to take the time to prepare your mind for this great spiritual adventure."

Harold made a point of telling his audiences that to bring about successful prayer in their lives demanded that they learn to make their minds clear. If they allowed their minds to be filled with fears and doubts, it would not be possible for them to relax, to make themselves receptive, and to exercise the degree of faith required to accomplish effective prayer.

Harold was firm in stating that we should never pray as "a duty, an obligation, or a habit."

"We've all seen people who make a ritual of getting a prayer over with as quickly as possible," he said. "Such rapidly mumbled prayers have no thought or feeling behind them. Nothing is accomplished by such prayers."

Over and over Harold stressed that it was the feeling behind a prayer, not the words thought or spoken, which gets through to God.

"You actually pray every time you have a deep desire for something, a strong yearning, whether you put it into words or not," he said.

And then he would remind his listeners of the admonition of Jesus: "When ye pray, use not vain repetitions . . . for your Father knoweth what things ye have need of, before ye ask Him."

⁓

Certain thoughts are prayers. There are
moments when, whatever the attitude of
the body, the soul is on its knees.
—VICTOR HUGO

⁓

Harold was adamant that it was never necessary to make a public display of how devout you are. He would often tell a story about a friend of his who seemed to make a point of praying loudly in public places, especially restaurants.

"He prayed loud enough so customers at nearby tables could hear him," Harold recalled. "Possibly he thought God would pay more attention to him if he demonstrated his faith in a public place.

"In my opinion, all he accomplished was to make his friends and family feel self-conscious and embarrassed. God would have heard him if he had only bowed his head and prayed silently."

In an interview with Brad, Harold discussed the vexing problem of those who pray but do not receive answers. He offered the following suggestions that might explain why a proper connection was not being made to God:

- There may be a lack of faith that what is being prayed for can and will be realized.
- Perhaps the supplicant has failed to make his or her mind a clear channel so that God's power is able to work through it.
- The supplicant may be permitting conflicts to arise in his or her mind due to fears, resentments, or doubts.
- There is an insufficient amount of power of feeling behind the prayers.
- The prayers are for something impossible to attain—or for something undeserved.

Seven Secrets for Successful Prayer

On numerous occasions, Harold Sherman generously shared his own Seven Secrets for Successful Prayer:

1. Remove all fears and doubts from your mind before you start to pray.
2. Make your mind receptive so it is prepared to receive guidance and inspiration from God within you.

3. Picture clearly in your mind what it is that you desire to bring to pass in your life.

4. Have unfaltering faith that with God's help what you are picturing will come true.

5. Repeat your visualization and your prayer every night until what you have pictured becomes a reality.

6. Review each day's activities and constantly strive to improve your mental attitude, so your mind can become a clearer channel tuned to the God within you.

7. Realize that if your thinking is right and if you persist with faith and put forth every effort in support of your prayer then that which you create in your mind must eventually come to pass.

⌒

Do not pray for easy lives, pray to be stronger men.—JOHN F. KENNEDY

One Nation Under God?

According to Garry Wills in his article "Religion: A Constant in American Politics" (*Utne Reader*, January/February 1991), "Practice conforms to profession. About 40 percent of the American population attends church in a typical week (as opposed to 14 percent in Great Britain and 12 percent in France). More people go to church, in any week, than to all sports events combined! Over 90 percent of Americans say they pray some time in a week. Internationally, Americans rank at the top in rating the importance of God in their lives."

In his book, *Under God: Religion and American Politics*, Garry Wills states, "Neither Jefferson nor Madison thought that separation of church and state would lessen the impact of religion on our nation. Quite the opposite. Churches freed from the compromises of establishment would have greater moral force, they argued—and in this they proved prophets. Religion has been at the center of our major political crises, which are always moral crises—the supporting and opposing of wars, slavery, of corporate power, of civil rights, of sexual codes, of 'the West,' of American separatism and claims to empire. If we neglect the religious element in all those struggles, we cannot understand our own corporate past; we cannot even talk meaningfully to each other about things that affect us all (and not only the 'religious nuts' among us)."

When I visited the United Nations in New York, I saw this beautiful prayer which is proudly displayed in a marble plaque visible as one enters the building.

THE UNITED NATIONS CALL FOR PRAYER

Man has reached a critical point in history, where he must turn to God to avoid the consequences of his own faulty thinking. We must pray, not a few of us, but all of us. We must pray simply, fervently, sincerely, and with increasing power as our faith grows. We must condition the world's leaders by asking God's Spirit to descend upon their hearts and minds. We must condition ourselves, each and every one, by asking God's help in living so that peace may be possible. We must pray in church, at home, on the train, while driving, on the job—and keep at it. Each of us is important now. The ability of every individual to seek divine help is a necessary link in the golden chain harmony and peace. Prayer is a dynamic manifestation of love by the concerned, reaching out for God's help for man. You can help change the world by your prayers and your prayerful action.

> Dag Hammarskjöld,
> At the Dedication of the Prayer Room
> United Nations
> Headquarters

Are We One Nation Under God?

In the past, the United States of America has considered herself to be "One Nation, Founded Under God," as we have been declaring when reciting the Pledge of Allegiance, in the Salute to the Flag. Take a dollar bill out of your wallet and read: "In God

We Trust"; in fact, all other U.S. currency proudly displays the same.

So why did I say "in the past," when it should read in the present tense, you remind me. It should. You are right. But is it true?

According to the results of the research and surveys I have summarized in this book, more and more Americans *are* realizing that "God" has been missing in the American dream, and more want to discover or rediscover "In God We Trust." More of us genuinely *want* to experience, firsthand, the power of prayer.

But many of us ended up putting our faith in the currency that carries the vow, rather than in the vow and commitment. Slowly, by the very process of daily living, we have become enslaved to the "almighty dollar" rather than set free by the "Almighty."

Now I'm sounding a bit preachy, and I certainly don't want to get into a major discussion of "religion" and/or politics, but there *is* something in this thought that has to do with the stress and the void that so many of us have pressing in on us.

It doesn't happen overnight. An old song goes something like, You work hard . . . and what do you get? Another day older and deeper in debt . . . Saint Peter don't you call me 'cuz I can't go. . . . I owe my soul to the company store!

It doesn't happen deliberately (not *always* anyway)! Inflation, the cost of living and the lifestyle that seems best for each one of us takes money—lots of money!

There is absolutely nothing wrong with money. It is the *love of money* that is considered a root of evil, scripturally. But today, the love of money doesn't even have to enter into the equation at all to be indebted *to* money.

We have all read the statistics and we know all too well from the frustrating experience that it takes both Mom and Dad to work in order to pay the bills and raise a family today. That in itself has been strongly instrumental in bringing about the great imbalance that exists in our society, with all its problems.

The mounting stresses of accumulated financial debt, the complete lack of enough *time* for family, children, and *oneself* are creating more problems than individuals, families, institutions, and yes, the government with the national debt, are able to deal with. The daily news reports remind us of the increase in bankruptcy, deceit, crime, disease, and in general people are unable to handle it anymore.

~

Live your whole life . . . as if it were a prayer.

~

What does this have to do with prayer? Several things: One of the very basic and fundamental lessons taught in each and every major religion is that in order to grow spiritually, to have inner peace, to know God, one must set aside time for prayer, to isolate oneself in quiet and solitude, to contemplate and reflect—or to "set thee" or "get thee" apart!

We barely have time to do a single thing out of the routine of our daily experience of school, work, and home, much less to set aside that kind of time. I hear complaints every day from hardworking, conscientious people that they didn't even get time to read the paper, much less find quiet time.

More than one mother and father go in the bathroom and close the door in hopes of finding some "quiet" for a few minutes, and not even that always remains uninterrupted!

Back to the basic question. Are we one nation under God? If America was founded on freedom of religion (for one thing), then why all the fuss and debate to keep prayer out of schools, business, and institutions? Does it make sense for a nation that puts God first on the printing of our currency, that salutes the flag, and sings the National Anthem with our hand over our heart, and recites "One Nation Under God," to suddenly not be allowed to even say a silent prayer at the start of each day?

Certainly, there are no "prayer police" to forbid us from saying prayers on our way to work or at work or school, or silently when we are there as long as we are unnoticed and it takes no time from our schedules!

Yet, school is the one place that teaches and sets an example. The example of our "National Declaration" seems suddenly to be limited to before a football game or such. The profession of "In God We Trust" and "One Nation Under God" seems to have been buried in politics and to be politically correct as we no longer can turn to the source of our strength—for strength! Now that's irony!

Why? What has happened? It seems that in the spirit of being politically correct and separating church and state the most basic and solid principle of *spirit* is being ignored, *and* the basic principle of *our country is being ignored!* What's next—to take off the currency, "In God We Trust"?

America is viewed by many Mideastern countries as the "harlot, the infidel"; yet a large faction of Americans look to the Mideasterners as the infidels. They pray at least five times a day. They don't allow movies, television, or print or advertising to bombard them with sex, booze, drugs, and violence. They don't allow lewd or suggestive dress and they don't tolerate lewd behavior. It is their religious beliefs that keep them from the same pitfalls that our religion warns against.

Don't we need to get back to a concern for teaching the religious values that our creed professes? What a tough issue. Freedom of the press and the airwaves is essential. What we are missing is the will of the individuals, each one of us, to refocus, re-aim, and hopefully unite in a common goal of serving God and one another.

⌒

Prayer is not an old woman's idle
amusement. Properly understood and
applied it is the most potent instrument of
action.—GANDHI, *Nonviolence in Peace
and War*

⌒

In giving voice to all religions for their individual
expression have we decided that none of them can
and none of us can say a generic group prayer?

Science is proving beyond a doubt that there is
tremendous power in group thought. The power en
masse is stronger than that of one. Most of us are
praying to and believe in One God. Maybe the particulars vary, just as does our own individuality, but it
is the central point that matters: We are a nation of
many people—many cultures, religions, and ways—
but what happened to "One God" and with liberty
and justice for all?

All the Holy Books teach that it is not just a once-
a-week church matter for religious and spiritual
growth. It must be a way of life.

It is as though the stage is set but who is directing
the play? So, to sum up, it seems like the advertising
and other distractions are all aimed at squeezing God
out of our lives. Doesn't it seem they are trying to
tell us that *all* other things are more important than
God, than spirituality?

In seminars and stress-management sessions I have

led around the world, I have demonstrated how the power of being of one accord, or of one mind, has a demonstrable physical effect. I have also demonstrated some fascinating experiments (some with double-blind control mechanisms) that show the immediate effects of prayer.

Just a thought: Perhaps if we started a day of work, if we study or work in a group situation, with five minutes of designated time for everyone to bow heads and go within to a silent prayer to the One God of our nation, with the simplest of instruction to pray to be and do the best we can with God as our "Guide," and to pray for help from above to treat each other as we wish to be treated (the Golden Rule of *all* religions), just perhaps the balance would come back to our lives.

Yogananda's World Prayer

Let us pray in our hearts for a League of Souls and a United World. Though we may seem divided by race, creed, color, class, and political prejudices, still, as children of the one God we are able in our souls to feel brotherhood and world unity. May we work for the creation of a United World in which every nation will be a useful part, guided by God through man's enlightened conscience.

In our hearts we can all learn to be free from hate and selfishness. Let us pray for harmony among the nations, that they march hand in hand through the gate of a fair new civilization.

Even from outer space to earth, invisible waves carry an astronaut's voice and pictures of what he/she is doing. On July 21, 1969, we were amazed to sit in the comfort of our living rooms and watch our little boxes with a viewing screen, showing us the "one small step for man, and the giant step for mankind," as astronaut Neil Armstrong walked on the *moon*!

It is possible now to see pictures from space during flybys of Jupiter! What was only fantasy and science fiction fifty or sixty years ago is now science *faction*. To me it is still a complete miracle that a part of me can be teleported magically from Forest City, Iowa, to Osaka, Japan, in less than one minute, via the amazing fax machine or the no less than amazing E-mail on the ever-growing and advancing computer!

In fact, there are so many new inventions and discoveries regarding these energies that surround us, that the education of the same lags way behind. Educators say that our current textbooks and lay understanding are at least ten years behind—and growing. New discoveries happen at a rate faster than we are able to synthesize them. So, for the purposes of this book, rather than elaborate on what my research has turned up in the realm of the incredible, I will attempt to write only about those most relevant to prayer.

We Actually Live in an Ocean!

We actually are immersed in an ocean of electromagnetic fields. These fields reach us in different wavelengths like ultraviolet, microwaves, and so forth. The different wavelengths change the polarity and capacity to act/interact/react of *all* other energy fields, including our own physical bodies.

East Meets West on Prayer

"Most men consider the course of events as natural and inevitable," the great yogi Paramahansa Yogananda once said. "They little know what radical changes are possible through prayer."

Realizing that most people consider the act of praying to be either vague or wishful thinking and turn to prayer only when tragedy or dire need besets them, Paramahansa Yogananda wished to teach as many as were willing to learn that prayer is real—and that there are actual scientific laws that govern it. As early as the 1930s, Yogananda was teaching that true prayer is based on the very precise laws that govern all of creation:

> Our physical bodies and the material world we live in are condensations of invisible patterns of energy;

That energy, in turn, is an expression of finer blue-prints of thought—the subtlest vibration—which governs all manifestations of energy and matter;

That God brought all creation into being by consciously willing His ideas to condense, first into images of light and energy, and then into the grosser vibrations of matter.

Yogananda declared that we, as human beings made in the image of God, have the freedom to use these same divine powers of thought and energy. In his view, prayer is actually a daily necessity in order to have harmonious living.

By the thoughts that we habitually entertain and act upon, we create the circumstances through which our life unfolds. Scientific prayer, then, is based on an understanding of this truth and an application of the universal forces of creation. Prayer is the modem through which we attune the human mind and will to the Divine Will of God.

If we patiently persevere in the application of prayer, we can, through God's unlimited power, love, and aid, dissolve all manner of difficulties and diseases for ourselves, as well as for others. We can, with the help of God, establish positive patterns of health, success, and receptivity on our subconscious minds.

As Yogananda once phrased it, "The human mind, freed from its disturbances and restlessness, is empowered to perform all the functions of complicated radio mechanisms—sending as well as receiving thoughts and tuning out undesirable ones." And, as he went on to draw a comparison between the radio and the human mind, he suggested that just as power of a broadcasting station ". . . is regulated by the amount of electrical current it can utilize, so the effectiveness of a human radio depends on the degree of willpower possessed by each person."

God builds his temples in the heart on the
ruins of churches and religions.
—RALPH WALDO EMERSON

An Illuminated Master, such as Jesus Christ, who attained self-mastery and perfectly attuned his will to the will of God, can "transmit" a divine power to accomplish instantaneous healings of body, mind, and soul. No matter how miraculous such healings may seem, Yogananda said, they are just the natural result of scientifically fulfilling the universal laws of creation.

Teaching as one of his basic tenets that any person who prays according to such principles will find that his or her prayers will also have a tangible influence—albeit, somewhat less authoritative than a Master—Yogananda originated the Self-Realization Fellowship Prayer Council and the Worldwide Prayer Circle, each dedicated to the upliftment of humankind through prayer.

Asked frequently how any single individual could

best affect positively the suffering in our troubled world, Yogananda's answer was always, "through prayer." War, poverty, disease, anxiety, lack of purpose in life—all these physical, mental, and spiritual maladies can best be addressed through the power of prayer.

"Only spiritual consciousness—realization of God's presence in oneself and in every other living being—can save the world," Yogananda said. "I see no chance for peace without it . . . It is your duty to do your part to bring God's kingdom on Earth. As the Master Jesus said, 'Greater things than these that I do, you can do . . . if you so believe!' "

Paramahansa Yogananda stated that it was possible to pray for others, especially if one requested that they "may be receptive to God and thus receive physical, mental, or spiritual help directly from the Divine Physician. This is the basis of all prayer . . . prayer heightens receptivity."

5

The Laws of
Physics and Prayer

How Much Do We Really See,
Taste, Touch, Smell, or Hear?

In 1976, during one of the courses I took in my *continual*—continuing education, I learned a most interesting, yet humbling fact: Scientists are saying that with all of our known human senses intact, we only perceive $\frac{1}{10}$th of 1 percent of all the energies that surround us. Just think of that! Is that telling us that most of life is passing us by or going unnoticed? If we only perceive $\frac{1}{10}$th of 1 percent, we are *missing* over 99 percent of life that surrounds us! How can that be possible?

Even that long ago (mid-1970s), new technologies

were detecting things we previously did not even know were there. We are surrounded by and literally immersed in an electromagnetic spectrum. Yet the only wavelength that is visible to the naked eye is the tiny little area between the infrared and the ultraviolet bands in the electromagnetic spectrum.

Scientists are constantly detecting and classifying these energies that surround us with sensitive high-tech equipment and instrumentation. As they are discovered, there await secrets locked within each of the fields of how they interact with our own, as well as how they can be tapped for developing technological applications.

For example, fifty years ago, had we ever heard of microwaves? Now, in 1997, a microwave oven is commonplace in most every home. The microwaves were there all along, but we first had to discover *that* they were there, *what* they are, then *how* to use them!

New discoveries continue to unfold and be developed of how microwaves can be utilized. In addition to cooking our food, microwaves are being used for sending and receiving communication.

We take radio and television for granted, yet they, too, have not been around all that long. Can we *see* the energy that is being transmitted into our television set that forms a picture? Can we see the energy that cooks our food in a microwave oven? Nor can we see what transmits our voices from phone to phone from one part of the world to another.

We Really *Do* Have An Aura!

It is not just a "New Age" lingo—we truly are surrounded by an aura. Each and every one of us has one all of the time! This aura is technically called a "biomagnetic field," or an electronic field.

In the midseventies, I had the pleasure of meeting two brilliant and fascinating authors, Lynn Schroeder and Sheila Ostrander. Together they researched and wrote about new scientific discoveries that at that time seemed to be much more advanced in other countries. Their books, such as *Psychic Discoveries Behind the Iron Curtain*, and *Superlearning*, were quite avant-garde and extremely informative and intriguing.

Lynn and I, in particular, became good friends and met on occasion. I was fascinated, as we often compared notes on our various thoughts and findings, how much their research overlapped with mine, yet from different sources. To me, what they called "psychic" or "extrasensory" perception (ESP) was the same basic thing as the religious "phenomenon" that I studied, just with different terms.

Actually, many of the researchers, authors, theologians, shamen whom I have studied with all agree that it is most unfortunate that we have to use terms or labels to define things. Sometimes it is the very definition of something that gets in our way of actually realizing the truth of it.

We need a way for our finite minds to grasp a concept by using words to describe or categorize it, but often the term itself becomes an alienator before we even examine the contents! I have found many people who are "fundamental Christians" (as they are labeled) are very offended by and advise all to stay away from anything "psychic."

In my own attempt to come to know why, I have learned there is a very good reason—for *some* aspects. But mostly, it is the term itself—no matter what it is—that is in the way.

For example, the word "aura" has the connotation to a fundamental Christian that it is of the occult. To a New Ager the term fundamental Christian might represent someone who judges them as wrong in their spiritual beliefs. In reality, if they dropped the label, often they believe basically the same thing.

Scientific Discoveries Could Bridge the Gap

This may sound far-fetched to those of you who are not familiar with these things. What many call psychic powers or discoveries is on the cutting edge of many of our understandings of energy and brain/mind/body science. Yet it is actually more than 2,000 years old!

Jesus performed many miracles that not only astounded and captivated the hearts and souls of his followers then, but still continue to gather millions and millions of followers and believers this many thousands of years later.

Before that even, Moses, Abraham, Elijah demonstrated the power and miracles of God. These miracles were always preceded by prayer. In the miracles of old, is there the science of the new? I think miracles are simply a term for a science we do not understand yet.

Jesus gave the admonition and proclamation that lies at the center of all. Jesus cast out demons that were afflicting and tormenting humans. Jesus was an alchemist, turning water into wine. Jesus cured the incurable of diseases such as the feared and contagious leprosy—instantly. Jesus defied the elements. He stilled a raging storm at sea. He walked on water from shore to board ship and quell the fear of his disciples at sea. He turned several loaves of fishes into a meal to feed 5,000 people. He told his disciples where to cast their nets to turn a fruitless fishing expedition into a burgeoning net, overflowing with fish!

There is only one religion, though there are
a hundred versions of it.
—GEORGE BERNARD SHAW

With all of these miracles and many more that are recorded that Jesus demonstrated that long ago, one of the most powerful points of His miracle demonstrations was and still is: that God loves and cares for all of his children. Another, and perhaps the point that becomes a "troublemaker" for many, is when Jesus said: "Greater than these things that I do, *you* can do—if you so believe!"

What about that? Why did Jesus say that if it were not so? How many of us feel as if we really can do *any* miracles that even come close to what Jesus did? Again, I think the word "miracle" is a science to be discovered. We are all so easily captivated by demonstrations of such miraculous types. Jesus gave us the formula for the miracles, but more than that, *the pattern for life itself!*

Again, the formula is in prayer. The truth is that it is not the person . . . it is God *through* us, God *in* us. "Greater is He that is *in* us, than he that is in the world." Miracles are something wonderful, but not the all that ends all. They are a gift. They are a sign. The something even *more* wonderful is the Spirit of God, the Spirit of Love that underlies the miracles and brings peace.

Jesus gave us the formula for the science of prayer, which we will examine. If one knew nothing else than this formula of prayer, contained in it is the secret of *peace on earth* and *peace of mind*.

To fully understand the teachings of Jesus, I have become convinced that we have to realize that all things are interconnected and interrelated. Each of us has a special place in the scheme of things and it is the grand and cosmic word, not only of Jesus, but of others who tell us to JUDGE NOT, so how can we put one faith over another faith or judge that our interpretation is right and another's is wrong? "By their fruits, you shall know them" and those fruits are fruits of the Spirit: patience, long-suffering.

My hope is that by integrating my understanding and study of the pattern of Jesus and unfolding laws of scientific discovery with my research, study, integration, and application of and with those of other paths, religions and ways—and sharing with you the outcome of as much as I can in this book, it will tie together many loose ends and unanswered questions that you might have that block your true power of prayer.

There is a golden thread of the power of prayer that has its anchor in science as well as in Spirit and it has been taught throughout the ages and the world, and is as powerful today as it was thousands of years ago!

But Is It Really New?

Strangely, this new reality turns out to be an old one—rediscovered. In my study of ancient traditions and primitive peoples and religious beliefs and practices, I have been most intrigued by the commonality of what I deemed to be one of the main focuses—and central teachings of them all.

In the late sixties, I was writing about what I saw and described as a "red thread running through the tapestry of all humankind." One of the most significant aspects of this red thread is their belief that religion and science were one!

The deeper one goes into some of the so-called primitive ways, an understanding emerges that is not so primitive after all. Laws of physics go hand in hand with ancient spiritual principles.

Newton's law—for every action there is an equal and opposite reaction—is the same as the first law of Eastern Philosophy, and the same as the foundation of Christianity or Judaism: The Golden Rule, "Do unto others as you want others to do unto you." This is the very foundation of religious *and* scientific thought.

As techniques develop, they do not become more complex, necessarily. Perhaps they become simpler. We can see the effects of this in a physical way with the use of a simple element found in nature—the quartz crystal. Advanced understanding of the crystal in liquid form has reduced the size of radios, computers, cellular phones, calculators, and virtually countless items shrunk to a mini-size.

The earliest computer took up a whole building; now the same or "increased" capabilities of that computer is down to the size of a television screen and box.

Sherry Hansen Steiger

The 100th Monkey
and Global Peace

In 1952, on the island of Koshima, a group of scientists from the Primate Research Institute of Kyoto University in Japan were studying the behavior of Japanese macaque monkeys. They noted that cultural differences occur within the same breed that live in different regions. For instance, the macaques that live in Takasakiyama throw away the hard stonelike pit found inside the fruit they eat from the maku tree; whereas the macaques from a different region of Arashi-yama break it with their teeth and eat the pulpy inside of the pit.

This might seem like an insignificant difference, you might be thinking. It could be likened to the difference between an Italian who eats spaghetti by twirling it around a fork, then guides it to his mouth with a spoon, and an Italian who cuts spaghetti with a fork and knife into more manageable bite-size portions. Although it would not matter in the least to most of us how one eats spaghetti, believe it or not, many Italians see a great deal of importance in this issue.

Our daughter Kari, who married an Italian and has lived in Italy for many years now, tells us this is a very significant issue there, and there is a "right" way and a "wrong" way to eat spaghetti, depending on where you live, and a great many arguments spring from it!

Now, although this seems far from relevant to prayer, and to world harmony, it isn't. Let me explain. Many religious doctrines that dictate the right way and the wrong way to do things, including "how to pray," believe it or not is like the Italian spaghetti etiquette. It's a *big deal* only if you are in an opposing camp! I can't imagine from a higher perspective, from God's perspective, that method has anything at all to do with it. Relating to prayer, it would be the heart and sincerity of the pray-er that God deems important.

For purposes of this book, the main point of the difference in eating methods of the macaques is actually what that discovery led to. In an effort to determine how behavior changes, spreads, or becomes indoctrinated in a species, a group of scientists put potatoes on the beach, on the island of Koshima, in hopes of attracting monkeys near the shore for closer and easier observation.

The scientists observed that the monkeys seemed to really like raw sweet potatoes, but they did *not* like it when the sweet potatotes were covered with sand, which these were, of course, because they were on the beach, so the sweet potatoes were not being eaten very fast.

Not interfering, the scientists simply observed how the monkeys would deal with this. The macaques might attempt to eat a sweet potato many times, apparently forgetting about the sand. They would also pick up others to see if maybe they were different, only to find the gritty sand or dirt so distasteful that they would lose interest.

Then one day, a young eighteen-month-old female macaque the scientists had named Imo found she could solve the dilemma of the dirty sweet potatoes by washing them in a nearby stream. Imo taught her discovery to her mother, then to her playmates, who also taught their own mothers.

Soon, over a process of time (between 1952 to 1958), and right before the scientists' very eyes, *all* of the young monkeys had learned this procedure of washing the grit and dirt off their sweet potatoes. They had learned that this process would make the sweet potatoes palatable.

The adult monkeys who did not learn from their children did not bother to wash the sweet potatoes; some of them even went ahead and ate them dirty.

Something mysterious occurred on one particular day, which has since come to be known as the "hundredth monkey phenomenon" (or syndrome). In the autumn of 1958, a certain number of Koshima monkeys were washing sweet potatoes. The exact number of monkeys is not known. Then, just as if some magical number had been reached, such as the *100th monkey* joining in to wash its sweet potato, almost all the monkeys, old and young, were washing their sweet potatoes!

The strangest thing is that *simultaneously,* colonies

of monkeys on other islands, and even the mainland troop of monkeys at Takasaki-yama, *all* began washing their sweet potatoes!!

It was magical and mystifying—almost as though a mass demonstration had taken place on some huge movie screen that was seen by all monkeys in separate places everywhere! How could this happen?

Breakthrough Discovery—Is there a Carrier Wave for Prayer?

Scientists speculate that perhaps when a certain critical number within a species achieves an awareness of something, this new awareness may then be communicated from mind to mind through the ethers.

The exact number may vary greatly for different concepts. In other words, if only a limited number of people or animals know of a new way, it might remain localized, and remain as the consciousness or property of a particular group.

But scientists say that there is perhaps a point at which if just one more person, animal, or living thing tunes in to a new awareness, a "field of thought energy" may occur that allows this awareness to reach everyone! In fact, all living things may communicate this way as well.

I am going to add to this some other research that I came upon about twenty years ago that I believe is relevant here as well. It has been proven that if one

Dutch elm tree, for example, on one particular street has contracted Dutch elm disease, then other Dutch elm trees in the area, even blocks away, put out a defense-system alert by releasing a certain chemical to the leaves. If a certain number of trees respond to the signal and release their own protective chemical, then most trees will *not* get the disease.

If for some reason the trees pick up a stronger "sick signal" of the diseased tree (or trees)—without getting its immune system's protective chemical released to the leaves—then most likely that tree and a whole lot of others, perhaps even *all* of them in the area, will probably get the Dutch elm disease, and die.

It is my theory that this applies to prayer as well. Perhaps there genuinely is a "carrier wave" for prayer. What if that certain magical number were reached with a unity of prayers, all with the same intent? If every day in schools, homes, and places of business, we silently said a prayer to God to help us all be more loving to God, ourselves, and to all others, do you think that the "carrier wave" would reach a mystical level just like it did with the macaque monkeys, and one day in the future we would awaken to a planet whose peoples treat all others with love and kindness?

Perhaps this is what Jesus meant when he said: ". . . if you have faith as small as a mustard seed . . . Nothing will be impossible for you." A tiny little mustard seed has within it the plan for the whole huge mustard plant. When the seeds are scattered by birds and the wind the plant is extremely quick to grow and spread.

When asked which of the commandments of Moses, or the things he taught, was the most important, Jesus answered: "You shall love the Lord your God with all your heart, and with all your soul, and with all your mind. This is the great and the first commandment. And a second is like it, You shall love your neighbor as yourself. On these two commandments *depend all the law and the prophets.*" Matthew 22:37–40

This teaching is a universal teaching. It is a universal truth. It is the same as the Golden Rule, which is found basically in all religions. I believe it could be as simple as that. That if that magical number of people prayed—believing, that it might be possible for harmony and the "kingdom of heaven on earth." Jesus also said: "The kingdom of heaven is *within you.*" In other words, that *seed* is within us to nourish, to grow to blossom and spread. But there is an *if*. It has to be of the *will* of each and every person, who is given the *free will* by a loving, not dictatorial God.

~ 6 ~

Can Prayer Affect the Weather and Other Questions about the Far-Reaching Effects of Prayer

Laugh if you will, but guess what the answer is? Although it might be very rare, the answer is yes, prayer can affect the weather. We know that the weather affects us, sometimes for the good—sometimes, not so good! On sunny days we usually feel a little brighter in our disposition and on rainy or dreary days, besides making our sinuses crazy, we might feel somewhat melancholy. And, I wouldn't be a bit surprised if we soon have evidence that shows *our* moods affect the weather.

There is no dispute either, that what we as humankind have done to the planet has altered the patterns of the weather. Pollution, stripping the forests, damaging the ozone layer, and on and on is not what I am talking about here.

I'm referring to miracles such as the time when Jesus calmed the raging storm at sea; or when Samuel called upon the Lord in prayer and the Lord sent thunder and rain that day, causing all the people to greatly fear the Lord and Samuel. (Old Testament, Samuel 12:18)

There are many amazing "weather miracles" that were recorded, many of them in the Bible, as a result of calling on God for help—in prayer—not for just "mood" reasons or for the king's parade!

The Prophet Elijah "prayed earnestly that it might not rain: and it rained *not* on the earth by the space of three years and six months. And he prayed again, and the heaven gave rain." (James 5:17, 18)

When catastrophic storms such as tornadoes, the devastating earthquakes and hurricanes wreak havoc with people's lives, their homes, their possessions, I feel so much pain and a sense of grief. This last year, Mother Nature has left towns in Florida looking like toothpicks from the air. Kobe, Japan, was left like a bomb had been dropped on the entire area; nearly completely destroyed.

In these and countless other cases, the ravages of weather came in too fast to be detected in order to give warning, and they left—just as fast, yet with catastrophe and heartache behind.

I know for a fact that the great evangelist Pat Robertson called for his viewers of the 700 Club television program to join together in prayer with him and the 700 Club staff, and plead with God to divert a great approaching storm that would have most likely wiped out Virginia Beach, or at least, done an incredible amount of damage, most certainly including the loss of lives.

As I followed the forecast, the storm was still aimed straight at Virginia Beach. No change. The prayers kept coming in, as Pat Robertson continued to lead viewers in prayer. Then just about at the eleventh hour and minutes until it was to hit—it changed direction! Miraculously, the storm turned and went out to sea, not doing harm to any other town, and not touching down in Virginia Beach!

My own miracle occurred one time when I decided to be bold and take a fishing boat out by myself, for a little contemplative time and to enjoy the beauty of nature. We had been on a tour with our Celebrate Life multimedia show, and were taking several days to camp and relax at the Louisiana Bioux, in New Orleans.

I was really enjoying the uniqueness of the low-hanging cypress with the Spanish moss just dripping off the trees, even at times into the water, they were hanging so low. The beauty lasted until a thought popped in my head to have my wits about me and make certain that a snake didn't jump off those low-hanging branches, onto me or in the boat!

Trying not to let that "caution" turn to fear and spoil my cruise, I realized that the water was getting rougher. Another thought popped into my head: What if the boat capsizes with these waves and an alligator gets me! Great! That thought was not welcome—at all!

I had managed to get quite far, in fact, I wasn't too certain where I was! It was so windy and twisty. The boat was a mere rowboat with a motor hooked up to the back, mainly for fishing. One thing I wasn't worried about was the boat. I felt confident that the person who sent me off in the boat had done a good job to determine I had all I needed for my outing.

The water kept getting rougher and the winds had picked up enough that they were actually pushing the boat, nearly doubling the speed. At first I thought it was great fun—until I saw that the massive Pontchartrain Lake was in view. I had been warned to "no way, no how" go that far—"it's too dangerous for this little boat."

Suddenly, the motor stopped. I tried and tried to no avail to restart it. Finally giving up, I unscrewed the top and looked into the can for the gas level, only to peer down at an empty bottom! I had been told I had enough gas to cruise around safely for hours! Ha!

The winds were blowing not only the boat, but it was as though they had some power to blow all those fear thoughts back into the forefront of my emotions—about alligators and snakes! I was getting scared. Not knowing me, you would not know that I usually do not get scared at all. I have done some extremely risky and dangerous (perhaps very stupid, even) things without fear. I *love* nature!

I calmed myself, and looked around for the emergency oars that I knew had to be there. Maybe there was a spare gas can with refill fuel. I found neither! Nothing was going to help me get out of this jam. The wind continued to gain force and momentum from behind me, as if some force was just blowing me out to danger!

I screamed out to God, "Please dear God, please get me back. Help me!" Almost at once, the wind completely changed directions. It literally did a 180! The wind instantly reversed directions—literally— inches from the big, big lake. Then it calmed and *slowly* blew me all the way back (almost to the very spot) where I left!

There was yelling along the way, as people were shouting out "there she is"! The word somehow got out that there was this little old lady (well, maybe not old!) out alone in the storm. There were calls out for rescue, but they didn't know if they could find me.

This was in the less sophisticated (technologically, anyway) '60s, so there was not the computer or eyes in the sky detectors back then. So, God answered my prayer with the miracle of reversing the wind! The alligators had to find their own supper, after all, and it wasn't going to be me!

To be fair, I'm sure you could be thinking as I have since, How do I know it was God answering prayer, maybe it was just a coincidence. Nothing wrong with that either, actually. The result, the benefit is still the same—safety!

But over the many years since that time, in my thinking and evaluating that and myriad other experiences, I think not. I'm not quite at the point where I believe completely that there is no such thing as coincidence; I think maybe sometimes there is. But most of the time I think there are actions we take and everything can be sort of like the domino effect—one sets off all the others in a flow of motion.

Sometimes the decisions we make set off a nice flow, other times one that is like a storm itself, wiping out the other dominoes on down the way, but then new ones pop up! Maybe this sounds a bit like Forrest Gump's "life is like a box of chocolates" theory, only Gump's makes more sense!

Truly, I do feel a sense of awe about the free will that we as humans have been given. Within that free will there seems to be a lot of latitude for divine intervention, at times. I felt this was definitely one of them!

Was Pat Robertson's experience with prayer heading off a potentially fatal hurricane a coincidence? I suppose it is possible that we could examine and label all things such, but in light of new research, it makes more and more sense to me, and I hope to you, that it is truly possible that intervention takes place, that God sends angels to rescue us or alter patterns of nature, or the weather, if the intent and the need is right?

Rolling Thunder Makes Rain

In *Indian Wisdom and Its Guiding Power*, as well as in several other books, I have written fairly extensively about one of the most amazing and powerful persons one could ever meet, Rolling Thunder. One of the most significant moments in my entire life is the moment when "R.T.," as he is affectionately called at times, singled me out of thousands at a crucial time in my life in the late '70s.

Rolling Thunder is an intertribal medicine man, shaman for both the Cherokee and the Shoshone tribes of Native Amerindians. His rare abilities and powers have been documented and *researched* by such noted institutions as the Menninger Foundation.

The power in his prayers has been not only documented in cases of extraordinary healings, but for bringing rain. Not in the sense of Indian make rain dance (although many of my experiences testify to that is definitely no joke—it can happen!); but Rolling Thunder has his own prayerful techniques.

Drs. Elmer and Alyce Green conducted a very extensive study on the voluntary control of internal states, through the highly respected and notable Menninger Foundation.

In *Science Year* (Chicago: Field Enterprises Educational Corporation, 1974), Drs. Elmer and Alyce Green give some of their findings based on their research of Rolling Thunder and others. They talk about a theory that a unique energy field, a "field of mind," must surround the planet (expressed in some aspects as electrostatic, magnetic, and gravitational fields) and each individual mind with its extension, the body, must have the inherent capability of focusing energy for manipulation of both INS and OUTS events. They state:

> Rolling Thunder has unusual powers of perception and of energy control. We also infer that the individual mind and the general "field of mind" meet in the unconscious. They say that most persons cannot perceive or control their own unconscious psychological processes, and in fact would not even be aware of this field of mind. They see it as an important clue that the persons who are most aware of their own normally unconscious processes are the ones who seem to be able to control their own nervous systems and physiological processes (heart, blood flow, brain waves, pain). Rolling Thunder also seems to have the greatest extrasensory awareness of others, and the greatest ability to generate OUTS events, that is, to demonstrate psychokinetic powers.

Out of a clear blue sky, observers and researchers

have seen that Rolling Thunder's prayers can eventually bring clouds and rain. The theories of INS and OUTS have a different scientific view today. They have been proven in physics with a new basis and different terms.

Basically, the latest research supports the biblical teachings—"Anything is possible through prayer!"

Can Prayer Affect Warring Nations?

Throughout the history of Mother Earth there has been a black thread running through just about all peoples and nations, weaving a morbid and sad tale of one of the most difficult-to-understand aspects of humankind. That is of war, religious wars.

Yes, religious wars, "in the name of God," have been fought throughout the centuries. Whole cities, and even whole nations have been entirely eradicated, in the name of God. History is full of examples where a city or a nation's leaders called upon God in prayer to be on their side and to help them win the war.

For example, the prayerful devotion of Don Alfonso Henriques, the first king of Portugal, and his special devotion and regard for the archangel, St. Michael, as well as for his own personal guardian angel, is a matter of historical record.

King Alfonso had conquered a nearly impregnable Moorish fortress of Santarem. Sometime later, under the command of the Moorish monarch, Albaraque, the Moors made a formidable attack on the city, in hopes of retaking their lost fortress.

As I wrote in *Angels Around the World:* "In spite of a severe injury to his leg, King Don Alfonso Henriques insisted on getting into a chariot and joining in on the battle." Henriques knew that because of his prayers to God the angels would be with him in battle. "The angels were with Henriques, as he saw an arm grasping a sword and also a wing over him . . . showing him that he was protected. It must have been a fierce battle, as the Moors fled in terror. The Moorish captives that were taken in the battle declared that they, too, had seen the Angel."

The king was so grateful that he founded a military Order called the "Order of the Wing" in honor of St. Michael and the Angels. To this day, Portugal still celebrates and honors the day that God answered their prayers and sent angels to assist them in battle!

All Things Are Possible

In his book, *The Wondrous Way of Life,* Brother Mandus of Great Britain's World Healing Crusade states that the scores of thousands of men and women who have attended their divine healing services know for a certainty that God answers prayer.

"At such services we pray in the name of Jesus Christ, as He taught us to do and realize the instantaneous response, because illness and pains disperse, often in a few moments," Brother Mandus writes.

While the sight of people who could hardly walk suddenly moving about with joints freed and pain dispersed is a marvel to behold, Brother Mandus affirms that the healing of the flesh follows the healing of the soul and constitutes a much greater miracle.

"During a service we consciously fix our minds on God. We pray in the name of Jesus Christ and know that in God's presence we become whole—first in soul, then in body. God is the reality that upholds our very existence. At the moment of physical healing we have really entered this inner kingdom of divine love and our Heavenly Father. . . ."

Brother Mandus states that Jesus, "the supreme authority on prayer," has promised us that through faith and prayer we may remove every "difficulty, disease, discord, or disaster that may confront us. Jesus, he reminds us, tells us again and again that we are to have only faith and believe that we will receive an answer to our prayers: "And all things, whatsoever you shall ask in prayers, believing, you shall receive."

"Here is no diluted theology, but a living truth that will make all men free. The words of Jesus Christ proclaim the truth that man can commune with God and receive answers to every need. [This] literally means that little man has at his disposal all the resources of the Almighty Father to heal and solve every individual and collective problem on Earth. . . . All things are indeed possible, conditioned only by the limits of our belief."

Can Prayer Fix Things?

Prayer for Broken Appliances

At this very moment you are probably chuckling to yourself about how crazy this sounds, just as I did when someone first raised this point to me over twenty years ago! And no, this isn't some new craze, like "junkyard prayers." When I was first asked if I thought it was possible to "heal a 'thing' " through prayer, I was not going to give such a ridiculous notion any of my already-spread-too-thin time! In fact, I wasn't even going to dignify the question with an answer. Still, the expression on my face revealed my feelings that God cares for people, not inanimate things.

Undaunted by my look of discouragement, this person, I'll call Jane, said she had a friend who could "heal" broken-down appliances like toasters, etc. through prayer. Jane even offered to take me to this woman's home to see for myself what I thought about these "miracle healings" when Emily prayed and laid hands on an item.

How quick to judge I had been. I am still not certain of the answer. There are many possible explanations, but let it suffice when I say that I definitely believe that there are no limitations to the power of God. Perhaps that even includes "things."

More things are wrought by prayer
Than this world dreams of.
—ALFRED, LORD TENNYSON

I took her up on it and went to talk with Emily, only to find her with quite a few people who had brought various broken-down appliances to have her heal in a most unusual and unorthodox repair shop! It was no big deal to Emily. She would quiet herself, in what seemed to me to be an energy-gathering meditation, then put her hands on the item, pray, and command it to work. My inquiring mind wondered if this was one of those "rigged" revival-type things in order to gain attention and a following. Right before my eyes, so-called toasters and the like that had not worked for years worked now when they were "healed."

Emily herself was about as unassuming a person as you'd ever want to meet. She demonstrated a love and concern for people and their problems that appeared to be genuine. She didn't want a following—took no money for her efforts, and just considered it a gift that God gave her to pass on in her desire to be of service to others. Emily was not well. She was nearly confined to her home because of severe asthma. Her breathing was so labored that one was shocked, with the degree of wheezing, to find her home and not in the hospital.

The friends of hers who were there told me many stories of Emily's healing things one after another—from coffeepots to cars—even an old broken-down refrigerator. One of the gals told me that she was extremely low on money and had one thing after another go wrong. Then suddenly her refrigerator stopped. With four little children and no way to buy a new refrigerator, this person called Emily, pleading for her help. Emily felt sorry for her friend and said she would pray over the refrigerator. Her compassion on this occasion even took her to this gal's house. "When I took one look at the refrigerator, I thought, *no way*," Emily told me. She said it looked to her to be an old junker that deserved to break down.

Her friend must have sensed what Emily was thinking, because she promptly reminded her by blurting out, "You know we don't have the money for a new one, what will we do?" Emily said a prayer out loud, while both of her hands were on the refrigerator, "God, I'm sorry for my weak faith in putting limits on your power. Nothing is impossible to you. Please make this refrigerator work."

The women saw nothing right away. They sat at the kitchen table and had tea and a few cookies before Emily was to go back home when all of a sudden they heard a little rattling noise and the refrigerator motor started up! Both ladies let out such a scream, they said they thought the neighbors would be over to see what was wrong!

So, who knows? Was it just a coincidence that perhaps they opened and closed the door of the refrigerator with such a jolt that it started? But if that were the case, wouldn't it have started immediately after the door closed? The power wasn't out anyplace in the house, or we might offer that as a possibility.

Emily told me that there did not seem to be any explanation for the times that these odd healings would take place. They did not always work. There were many times that *nothing* would happen, but she learned not to doubt herself. She knew that it was *not* of her doing, but the power of God's love and energy "through" her. When the healings did not work, she did not question God.

Oddly, this same capability did not seem to work on humans. Although she'd been asked often to heal friends and herself, she told me that sometimes animals, but mostly appliances, were her thing. Sadly, Emily had even more health problems than she realized and it was only about a year until she succumbed to a very serious radiation treatment that wasn't enough to cure her. God called her home.

I often wondered about these things. I saw and heard for myself that Emily had this unusual gift, yet this had been rare indeed. In times of desperation, I found myself praying out loud for a few things here and there, not really with the belief at first, but more out of agony! Then several things happened that made me wonder even more. . . .

Prayer for Cars That Won't Start

Can prayer affect such things?

On one occasion while I was living in Denver, Colorado, my car would not start. I imagine that most people feel at such a time, no matter what the circumstances, that it is "urgent." I had no other car, no auto service card to call for help, and cellular phones weren't an option for the public at the time. Winter in the mountains is not the time anyone would opt to have such an experience, as if we had a choice in such matters!

There was no time to spare. As a matter of fact, it *was* a downright emergency for my state of affairs. I had left counseling and the ministry and I was working as a writer in a large advertising agency in Denver. They were a real stickler for being on time. I'd been separated from my husband for a time and was on my own, without financial help from anyone, and had sole custody of my daughter.

From the house I was renting it took me up to forty-five minutes to get to work, including taking my daughter to preschool, and that was if the weather and traffic cooperated!

I couldn't afford to be late—not today! I already had been late too many times with car trouble. It was driving me crazy (no pun intended—maybe that is where that expression came from!). I was not in a situation to be able to do anything about getting a new car and the money I'd "thrown away" to mechanics who kept fixing the same problem, again and again, was draining me even more.

Every time I was late it felt like my job was on the line. I was by far the youngest employee and had the definite feeling that every eye was watching my every move. Each day there were probably ten or more job applicants, eager to have my job, and they were all more qualified in advertising background and experience than I.

Something inside was letting me know, by the size of the knots wrenching my stomach, that if I could not get the car to start and was late today, it would mean my job. The more I tried to start the car, the worse the car seemed to get. As my inner tension grew, suddenly I heard that still small voice within say, "don't panic—remember Emily."

I sat there a minute or two, realizing that now I had flooded the car and had little choice but to wait. Then I thought to myself, what *if* there is some kind of energy or mind link that I could focus on the engine . . . or something. What did I have to lose? I took several real long, slow, deep breaths, then with real conviction, and out loud, said a prayer. While I was saying the prayer I was focusing energy as if it were a beam from a flashlight coming from my forehead and beaming out onto the engine of the car. It really felt as if this focused energy was a tangible thing coming from my forehead—I could almost *feel* it!

Now, I had already tried starting the car about twenty times, with no luck at all. Thinking I could have flooded it, I would wait a while then try again—still with no luck. Somehow, after this prayer and "focusing" I just had a feeling it would work—and it did!

Trying not to analyze why, how, and what . . . I just thanked God out loud and set out to take Melissa to preschool. This was not the first demonstration of the Power of God, nor the first of answered prayer; not by any means. It was, however, the first of a series of God's demonstrations to me that nothing is too petty or menial to call out a prayer, as long as there is a real need, not want—there's a difference.

Despite my previous concern over the triviality of inanimate things versus spiritual things, and although all the other troubles with my car were "urgent" I didn't want to bother God with my "technical" difficulties! There were people all over the world with *real* trouble and real pain. God was needed everywhere, and my troubles weren't worthy of taking His time away from the more serious matters.

But this time I actually allowed myself to call out in this kind of need. You've heard the saying, "Desperation is the mother of invention," well, it can also give us the opportunity to ask for help when I was used to doing everything for myself. That *by itself* often offers a lesson.

No effort is complete without prayer—
without definite recognition that the best
human endeavor is of no effect if it has not
God's blessing behind it.
—MAHATMA GANDHI

Some other thoughts on the subject come from Yogananda. He lovingly explains in *Autobiography of a Yogi* "It is all right to pray to God for things. It is better still, however, to ask that His will be done in your life. He knows what you need, and will do much more for you than the best that you can imagine for yourself!

"Above all, seek Him for Himself, for His love. Pray to Him, 'Father, reveal Thyself!' If you call to Him in that way, sincerely, He will be with you always.

"Never pray with the attitude of a beggar. You are God's child. As His child, you have a right to the treasure from His storehouse of infinity.

"If your heart is restless with desires, pray to Him,

'Lord, I have these desires, but I want You more than anything else. Help me to dissolve every limitation in Your great ocean of peace.''

Do We Place Limitations on God Answering Our Prayers?

Most of us grow up thinking of God somewhat like a huge person with magnified ability to do all things and be everywhere. And although invisible to us, from that cloud or wherever, up there He might be, it seemed like maybe there must be some kind of number system worked out in order to fit in everyone's requests. Sort of like you say a prayer and it rings a magic bell for God's attention. Instead of only waiting on one person at a time, maybe this unlimited Power could handle a million at the same time! Our finite minds struggle to understand the Huge concept of the Divine.

I hadn't realized that even though I was now an adult and had been engaged in uncountable theological discussions and debates most of my life. Then even at seminary, for heaven's sake, with other pastors, theologians, etc., yet these talks, debates—whatever or whoever—whenever it came to trying to grasp God being there for ALL of us, creating and caring for all creation, nobody could explain it.

It is ineffable. There's that wonderful feeling in your heart that God loves us ALL and will care for

us if we ask in prayer, but the head gets left out . . .
"don't think . . . believe!"

Suddenly I was made aware that I still had a
strong carryover feeling of "not wanting to be a
bother." Not to anyone really, but especially not to
the "Guy in charge"! It suddenly struck me how
much we do put personal attributes into our theology
about God. Limitations. We may have them, but God
has none! How can all of our prayers be heard? There
are *billions* of us on the planet.

In the vastness of space there could be billions of
planets with other life needing God as well. I became
aware that this might be the most difficult for all of
us questioning human beings to grasp—to understand. Even the best of my pastor friends and professors gave the classic "we have to take it on faith"
answer. I had too much of an inquisitive mind.
Things had to make sense to me. I would read, contemplate, study—and try to figure them out. Faith . . .
sure, I felt my faith was extremely strong. My faith
carried me through. But then there is *the faith* that
soothes the questions unanswerable—I didn't have
that.

Somehow, it just feels like an instinct we all might
have within, to know the real urgent from the trivial.
When I have exhausted all means possible to deal
with such situations, and it *isn't* an emergency, then
usually help appears. This is, of course, another way
God answers prayer. A trucker might stop and offer

help, or a passerby, if it's on the highway, or any number of other ways that God works through other people or other Divine means.

⁓

Prayer is the most tremendous power in the world!—NORMAN VINCENT PEALE

⁓

There was more than one occasion when similar miracles happened with me and my car troubles. In fact, they happened enough that my daughter, who was about three years old at the time, began to think nothing of such things. She would just say rather matter-of-factly, "Mom, just pray and focus energy and it will start. Why are you so upset . . . just do it!" Out of the mouths of babes, right?

I still astound myself at our human fallibilities and lack of faith. Certainly, I have had the blessing of the demonstration that prayer works, but there seems to be a much higher purpose and plan at work as to when and how it works. I never want to take for granted that I know the plan—I don't.

If prayer does *not* work, things will *always* work out.

There again, there have been times when it has *not* worked, but generally something always "works out." There is a difference. It is in that where I place my faith.

I think we all have many miracles and Divine intervention that perhaps because of our increasingly busy and complicated lifestyles and pressures we may tend to "forget" when the next crisis occurs. There is a real peace that occurs within us—once we learn to trust God, and *know* that things will work out.

God doesn't forget us—we forget God! The next time some unsettling event stresses you out and you start to feel anxious, take a few deep breaths and remember a time when you called on God for help—and everything worked out.

The more we can train ourselves to do this, the sooner the reality of Divine Law and Order becomes a part of our knowingness. God's love is *always* there for us. It is a matter of learning to trust and believe in that. Then our faith brings with it more and more miracles and more and more peace.

Trusting in God has been a part of our human dilemma since the beginning of recorded history. Struggling with faith has been a part of the lives of nearly all of the prophets and the saints, so why should we think we would not be vulnerable as well.

Archbishop Francois Fenelon, a French classic mystic from the seventeenth century, sums up a process of prayer for when we just can't seem to "get into the spirit" of prayer. There are many times that we all go through a little "down" period, even those of us who usually have no trouble expressing our soul in prayer. Francois must have experienced moods of spiritual and emotional deprivation—just like the rest of us as He guides us in such times:

Tell God your troubles, that God may comfort you;
Tell God your joys, that God may sober them;
Tell God your longings, that God may purify them;
Tell God your dislikes, that God may help you conquer them;
Tell God of your temptations, that God may shield you;
Show God the wounds on your heart, that God may heal them.
Lay bare your indifference to good . . . your instability.
Tell God how self-love makes you unjust to others, how vanity tempts you to be insecure, how pride disguises you to yourself as to others.

Our friend Beverly Hale Watson echoes many of our sentiments in her beautiful poem:

Hear Me Please

When troubled times ascend upon you
Do not fret and become despaired
For out of turmoil peace will come
If you'll rely on the mighty Son.

He has your answers . . . every time
If you will sit and silence your mind
Your heart projects the feelings of the Holy Spirit
While Divine guidance is given through intuitions.

Don't run in circles that have NO end—Instead

Believe in the wisdom of the Master . . . your Friend.
He can dry your tears and bring you peace within
When sorrow overshadows and hope seems dim.

God can light the way on your darkest days
Present opportunities that open doors when all else
fails
He is your "In House Counselor" who charges no
fees
His advice is simple: Have Faith; Listen; Follow Me!

⌣

By prayer and petition, with thanksgiving,
present your requests to God.
—PHILIPPIANS 4:6

7

Prayer Heals
a Crushed Hand

There wasn't much time to spare. As usual, I was working overtime. Although it was a forty-five-minute commute to and from work, circumstances were such that I needed to make the drive home in order to take my five-year-old daughter, Melissa, and the baby-sitter to get some dinner, and then go all the way back.

Oftentimes, I would take Melissa back to work with me for a while, or bring work home, but in this case, Sarah, the sixteen-year-old baby-sitter, was able to stay later, and I had a few things to pick up in that end of town for the meeting anyway, so I promised a brief but "fun" little outing for the girls.

Sarah said she would have Melissa ready, and they would watch out the window for me to pull up in the car. Sure enough, they were sitting on the porch steps and came excitedly to the car as I pulled up to the curb.

This was the first time Sarah had been in this car. My little Fiat Spider convertible was being fixed and I had a company car. It was quite different for the girls, as it was a very large sedan. It had been custom-ordered for me—and it had just arrived that very day. I knew part of the excitement for the girls in our little "fast-food" picnic outing was to see and ride in the new car!

Noticing that both Sarah and Melissa seemed to be taking a little more time than usual to get settled enough in their seat to fasten their seat belts, I decided Sarah was perfectly capable of closing the passenger door herself when they were ready. I walked over to the driver's side, got in, and turned on the ignition.

Melissa seemed settled on Sarah's lap, the seat belt was secured around them both; but the car door was still open. Sarah was raving about how neat the car was, and simultaneously, Melissa, too, was so thrilled that she kept saying, "Is it really ours, Mom?" Giving a wink, I kind of nodded toward the passenger door, in hopes Sarah would get my silent message to close the door so we could go.

Sarah gave a big smile, as if to acknowledge the silly oversight of an open door. She reached out, grabbing the handle of the big door, slamming it shut hard, and I took off down the street. Shocking me to the very core, Melissa let out the loudest bloodcurdling scream I had ever heard in my entire life.

"What's wrong?" both Sarah and I asked, and asked again, as Melissa just continued to scream with her face completely red and covered with extreme agony. Thinking maybe the seat belt was pinching her all of a sudden, or that Sarah moved and caught something on Melissa somewhere, I felt helpless. So did Sarah apparently, as she couldn't seem to locate the problem, either. Meanwhile, the screaming was growing even more intense, so I put on the emergency signal and pulled over to the side of the road to figure out what went wrong.

The frustration of the unknown source of pain kept Sarah asking Melissa what was wrong, which just seemed to intensify the screaming. Every time Sarah would try to move slightly, it got worse. Finally, my eye caught the source of the problem. Melissa's hand had been shut in the door!

I desperately tried to communicate to Sarah to open the car door. I pointed, I screamed out—all to no avail. The chaos of the screaming and pain in the air left total confusion, and I could see that Sarah was just not understanding what I was trying to get her to do.

Opening the door on my side, I raced around to the other side, opening the door. Melissa's hand was completely crushed—flat as a pancake. Near panic with anguish at my daughter's suffering, I tried to be as calm as possible, getting back into the driver's seat and heading straight for the nearest hospital emergency room.

Pulling into the emergency room entrance, I parked the car right in front of the door, knowing that I would have to come out and move it, but there wasn't time to drive around and look for a parking place. Getting out of the car, I went around and opened the door, taking Melissa carefully from Sarah's lap, and ran into the emergency room. Fortunately, once I made eye contact with one of the staff, holding up Melissa's arm, she instantly dove into action, rather than making me go through all the ninety-nine questions at the desk.

If you do not pray, everything can disappoint
you by going wrong. If you do pray,
everything can still go wrong, but not in a
way that will disappoint you.
—HUBERT VAN ZELLER, *Praying While You Work*

The doctor was a very caring woman who reached over to take Melissa from me in order to take her to X-ray. Melissa complained even louder (if that was possible), reaching out with her other hand for Mommy. She was soon out of sight, but not sound, when an attending physician approached me to fill me in.

I had already told them that Melissa's hand had accidentally been shut in the car door, but the attending physician added the prognosis. "Your daughter's hand is flatter than I have ever seen before. How long was it stuck in the door? It appears that all her fingers are broken—the thing is, there are a lot of other little bones in the hand, too. We'll have to hope that because she is so young that the cartilage is still pliable, and that there isn't splintering of the bones," he added.

He no sooner got the words out, not even pausing for an answer in between, than the baby-sitter burst out into tears like she *finally* understood what had occurred!

"I'm sooooo sorry, I'm so sorry," she kept repeating. "That was so dumb of me! I shouldn't have been jabbering. I should have been paying closer attention! Please forgive me! Oh my gosh, it's all my fault," Sarah kept on. She became so upset herself that I thought she was going into hysteria!

I assured her with a big hug, and tried to comfort her while she "dealt with it." She cried and cried, so I continued to pat her on her back—still hugging her until she understood that I was not blaming her. Once she calmed down, we tried to piece together how it happened.

"I thought Melissa's hands were both in. It never even dawned on me," Sarah grieved. We talked about how this car had a post in between the front and the back door, and either Melissa was still holding onto that, or . . . ? At any rate, I told her that whatever happened, happened. It was over and done with, so now all there was to do was to pray.

Just then, a nurse was wheeling Melissa back to the emergency room and into the examination room where they had us waiting. Melissa was, of course, still crying. By now her voice was so irritated from the screaming that she was sounding hoarse. I grabbed my purse and told Sarah to start digging through it to try and locate a cough drop or a piece of candy or something for Melissa's throat.

The nurse and attending physician put Melissa on the hospital bed from the wheelchair. I went to her, giving her a hug and a kiss, telling her that the doctor would fix it and make it all better soon. That sure didn't seem to assure her at all, but as I said it out loud, I realized that I was saying it more probably to appease myself and Sarah!

Melissa's unceasing agony was piercing my heart. Looking at her crushed little hand, I turned to Sarah and said let's pray over her hand. Sarah said she had never really prayed before and asked what to do. Telling her that I would pray out loud, and she could join me silently to help Melissa, I further explained for her to hold her right hand alongside mine over Melissa's.

"We are just going to put all our worry and fear to God and ask for help and healing. Just think about how much we both want her little hand to be all better, and picture in your mind like God is sending us energy through our hands—to hers," I said. Then we bowed our heads as I prayed intensely, releasing my anguish to God in pleading for Melissa's little hand to be healed.

All of a sudden Melissa stopped crying. It was such a complete shock to abruptly have quiet, and it came just about the same time I said Amen, that Sarah and I looked at each other first, then at Melissa. Then Sarah started to cry again.

Just at that moment, in walked the doctor! "Just as we thought, her fingers are all crushed. The X-rays are being read now, but I've already called in a surgeon," she said, as she gently touched Melissa's arm with a slight love pat and looked at her hand.

In one synchronized yell, we all blurted out, "Oh, my God, what happened?" Her crushed little hand had magically "puffed" out and was getting some color back to it. It was totally unbelievable. Moments before it had been so smashed flat that it was unimaginable how it could be fixed! Once again, the doctor asked, "Am I more tired than I thought? Is it her other hand?" Then realizing that she was looking at the right hand and it had been healed, she exclaimed joyfully, "It's a miracle, it truly is a *miracle!*"

Sarah was stunned. I was so elated myself to see right before our eyes this dramatic change—in the blink of an eye, literally. We had just closed our eyes to pray, opened them again to see a *miracle!*

As the doctor put on a metal splint just to keep

Melissa's hand immobilized, so it wouldn't get irritated and could continue to mend, Sarah turned to me with a big hug, saying: "Tell me more about prayer!"

8

Teaching Children to Pray

I have always treasured the memories of my childhood nightly prayer sessions. While I was growing up, I was fortunate to have someone tuck me safely into bed each night and stay with me and my younger Aunt Cheryl until we had each recited our prayers. Either my mom, grandma, Grandpa Johnson, or my Aunt Del would say to us, after tucking in the covers, which "secured" us, "Okay, now say your prayers."

Those were always comforting and reassuring words to hear. They seemed to give a kind of meaning and order to life—making all right with the world, no matter what had occurred that day. Sometimes Cheryl and I would say our prayer in unison, and then we would each have our special list of people to pray for. In the innocence of our youth, there was never a question as to who we were praying to—or that any possibility of not being heard or answered existed. There was simply the trust and openness that there was a God who loved and cared for us and listened to our prayers.

Perhaps that is the kind of thing that Jesus meant when he said that we should be as a little child: "Except ye be converted, and become as little children, ye shall not enter the kingdom of heaven" (Matthew 18:3). Here, converted means to change direction—change your ways. It is telling us to have the faith and innocence of a little child in terms of trusting and believing God.

In the book of Matthew we read that mothers are bringing their children to Jesus for him to lay his hands on them and pray. When the disciples, probably thinking they were doing a good thing, told the mothers and their children to leave, Jesus chastised them. More than likely the disciples were thinking that the children were too young to sit quietly and listen to the master. Perhaps they even thought this to be an imposition and a waste of their master's time. Jesus demanded that the disciples let the children stay and, further, to allow others to come. "Suffer little children, and forbid them not, to come unto me: for of such is the kingdom of heaven."

The book of Proverbs in the Old Testament tells us that it is our duty as parents to teach our children in the matters of spirit. Proverbs 22:6 says, "Train up a child in the way he should go, and when he is old, he will not depart from it." If all parents obeyed this, it would not be long until we had a harmonious world of children who have grown up with solid understandings and actions based on spiritual doctrines. Once again, the basics of all religious teachings are the same: promoting and putting God first and loving and honoring all as we so desire to be treated.

My First Prayer

The first prayer I was taught to recite at bedtime was the one that most others seem to have learned as well. Now I lay me down to sleep,/I pray the Lord my soul to keep./If I should die, before I wake,/I pray the Lord, my soul to take. That prayer never bothered me until I first was teaching it to my son, Erik. I caught myself, literally in the middle of the prayer, feeling surprised at my negative reaction to it.

It dawned on me that this prayer gave me the same feeling I had when I began singing or reciting nursery rhymes to him as an infant. That feeling was one of "What negative and downer words!" Remember "rock-a-bye baby" with the tree limb breaking and the baby falls down, *cradle and all?*

In one way, I saw nothing wrong with the Lord taking my child's soul. But to say this every night seemed to me to emphasize a scary thought that death was possible that very night.

One of my most valuable spiritual lessons was taught me by my own young son at a later point when he died early in life. That lesson was to love and treat your family members and those closest to you as if you won't, or might not, see them ever again.

If some misfortune should take them from you, and this is the last day you have with them, how would you treat them? Looking at all of life that way is really the greatest gift I could imagine to learn deep down. Only then are we really truly living life each day to its fullest. Treating each day and all our loved ones and others in this manner *also would make a harmonious world!*

However, I realized that more needed to be communicated in the prayer taught to *my* children. I wanted them to have the balance of an understanding of God's love for us, not a feeling of death lurking nightly—under the bed or in the closet or in the shadows on the wall or ceiling!

I have had hundreds of requests for the prayers that I taught my kids and others through church school education and counseling. So I will share both some guidelines with you and some of the prayers as well.

In my belief that prayer is a desired attitude and state of mind, that it is the ideal to strive for *all of the time,* I wanted to instill more than teaching just a prayer to my children. I observed that left to their own resources, children have a tendency, as we all do at times, to isolate one negative occurrence from a day of normal events and dwell on that. So in starting the nightly bedtime prayer with Erik, I addressed this by trying to focus at first on the good things that happened to him that particular day.

Seven Steps to A Prayerful Attitude Sherry's Bedtime Prayer Guide for Children

First, read a story from a book or make up a little story once you have tucked in your child or children. It does not have to be very long, and can vary in length with the time available. This quality time spent with you will mean more to your children than you could ever know.

This is also an opportunity to teach values and morals to the children through books that have been especially selected by you. There are many wonderful books that focus on virtues and spiritual teachings just for children, and of course there are the many old classics as well.

Bedtime is not always an event that children look forward to. This has never failed for me. It even provides an incentive for kids to have their bath and room picked up or whatever chores they might have—for them to complete those tasks in order to have time for the story. There may be times when you allow a choice, between a TV show or the story, if something extra special is on for a holiday (like a Charlie Brown special, etc.).

Second, if you don't have the time for a story, find some kind of a "warm fuzzy" to draw you and your child close to each other while tucking him or her into bed. This can be a favorite teddy bear or bunny, blanket or any snuggly, maybe even a puppet. I found that using the teddy or a puppet to tickle, give a kiss, talk like Mickey Mouse—or some playful but endearing and fun communication—serves as an extra special way of adding a light and loving touch to the end of the day's activities.

This is great to do as an addition to reading or telling a story if possible. This really works to make bedtime more enjoyable, plus it lightens up both yours and the child's attitude. It's amazing how such a small thing that does not take long can do wonders! Children actually begin to look forward to this special time.

"Now, let's say our prayer." To start with, it is helpful if you say some of it *with* your child. Start by saying simply: "Dear God, thank you for this day and for all of the good things that happened today."

Then pause and ask your child to remember out loud some of the good things. (It's astounding what you can learn!) If "nothing" is the answer you get, encourage at least one memory—no matter how seemingly insignificant, such as playing with friends, a special activity at school, the teacher was extra nice, etc. Help your child to develop an attitude of thankfulness for all things that normally we take for granted.

It is not important to name everything, although if time permitted, I often encouraged my kids to recall as many things as they could in order to get into the spirit of it. It is often helpful to draw out some observations, such as: did you notice anything special in nature, such as a pretty bird song, a squirrel looking for food, a beautiful tree with leaves changing colors, etc. If it is a gloomy, rainy day, encourage a thankful thought for rain to give a drink to the plants, trees and flowers (find the good in as many things as possible).

Then say, "Please help me, God, with the things that were not so good." Have your child mention a few of these. Encourage your child to be honest, but not to go on and on with the bad things. Allow just enough to ask: "God help me understand these things and show me what I can do to make them better."

If it happened to be a day that did not go so well,

I always would add, "Please help me make tomorrow a better day."

"Teach me to find ways to make others happy."

"God bless Mom and Dad (sisters, brothers) . . ." or just say "my whole family." Add anything particular for healing (body/mind/spirit), like help Sally get over the flu, etc.

"God bless all those who don't have anyone to pray for them. Amen."

This will soon develop into a habit with the pattern of thought finding a balanced focus in all of life. It might take ten minutes to a half hour; but there is nothing more valuable, in my opinion, if your time is of a premium, that you can give to your children—and it is free!

Ancient Teachings of Prayer

It wasn't until Erik had passed on and Melissa was just about grown that I was blessed to experience other cultural teachings in prayer. These were the closest to my own beliefs and those that I taught my children—that I developed simply because they made sense to me. There is usually nothing new under the sun, and I discovered for myself the beginnings of the real essence of spiritual teachings is not found in dogma, in seminaries . . . but from within.

I was pleased to learn from dear Grandmother Twylah, repositor of wisdom for the Seneca tribe, how the ancient Seneca taught their children to pray at an early age. They would pray in the spirit of thanksgiving. This was their first introduction to "going into the silence," as they call it. This is the method for seeking self-development and offering proper prayers.

The children were instructed that prayer was a creative process that began with an idea. Prayer must be accompanied with feeling. You cannot have prayer without having a definite idea accompanied with feeling. In order to have a prayer fulfilled, it is necessary to understand the levels of feeling. This understanding must exist before desires and actions can be controlled.

One of the first things that Seneca children learned was that they could create their own world, their own environment, by visualizing actions and desires in prayer. A child will create his own world through imagery. He will create his own environment. This is a natural gift with which we are all born.

~

For God alone my soul waits in silence.
—PSALMS 62:5

~

The Senecas believed that everything that made life important came from within. Prayer assisted in developing a guideline toward discipline and self-control.

From Rolling Thunder (one of the most important people in my life), I learned a great deal about the Native American attitude toward prayer. The reverence for all of life and the prayerful attitude that is taught is the closest to what I believe Jesus taught.

When Rolling Thunder picks an apple from a tree, or when gathering his herbs to use in healing, he always gives thanks. Before picking an apple, he gives a silent thank-you even to the tree from which the apple came or a thank-you to the bush from which the herb was picked. He would give something in return, something that would nourish the tree.

The thank-you is always ultimately to the Great Spirit, or God, or the Great Mystery, but I found the little thanks to the trees and bushes was so beautiful. I remembered that I often had done that on my own, sometimes out loud, starting when I was very little. No one taught me. I just would feel the sense of "miracle" that was there. Even when picking a flower, I say thank-you to the plant for its beauty.

The Native Americans also have that attitude when they take a life for food. That understanding of the give-and-take, the sacrifice animals, and the cycles of life are among the holiest I have witnessed. When on the hunt for rabbit, deer or other meat, a prayer is always said. "Thank you, rabbit, for providing nourishment to my people." That is a far cry from the mass butchering done in slaughterhouses today. Their belief that you take in the spirit of the kill, or you are what you eat, has much truth.

"Kill nothing with malice, but only love and grati-tude." "Take only what you need and waste noth-ing." "Give something back when you take." If a deer is killed, they use everything, including the hide for clothes, shoes, and many other things. We may have once all had that spirit and shared these actions, and I pray we all develop them again.

I have discovered in my research over the years a great deal of data that scientifically has shown that we do take in the spirit of the kill. If an animal suf-fers when it is killed, a panic and horror shoots chemicals throughout its body, just as when we get stressed our body releases harmful chemicals that were handy for "fight or flight" at one time but now are poisons and toxins to us.

These spiritual attitudes and teachings along with the counterpart in the physical have also been taught over the centuries by the Jewish (kosher food) and Muslim and many other faiths. We are now dis-covering that they are not silly superstitious myths or phobias, but have their merit—on all levels.

In the stress-management seminars that I have taught all over the country since the seventies, I dem-onstrate that there is a power that prayer can actually have on your food and its value to your health and your system. Saying a prayer before we eat has actu-ally been proven in laboratories, believe it or not, to make a positive difference in the amount of benefit one gets from the food one eats.

☙ 9 ❧

A Dying Child That Medicine Couldn't Cure Saved by the Power of Prayer

I was told of an amazing story after I had established The Butterfly Center for Transformation, a nonprofit healing center to which I had dedicated years and years of dreaming, planning, and researching before it became a reality in the early '70s. The center got to the point where there were forty different teachers working for me. Each one of them had a special aspect of expertise that added to the transformation and healing of body, mind, or spirit. One of the teachers relayed this dramatic true case that happened to a friend.

Dr. Martha Williamson's young daughter was hospitalized with a very, very serious fever. Little eight-year-old Jenny had a fever of 106 degrees that would not seem to break. She had been diagnosed with a rare virus that had infected and inflamed her brain and spinal cord. That high of a fever is not only life-threatening, but it can literally burn up brain cells, possibly causing severe brain damage.

From the neck down, Jenny was paralyzed on her right side. She seemed to be losing the battle to bring the blazing fever down and her whole body was fiery hot. As if this weren't enough, little Jenny would go into continual convulsions that would further ravage her tiny little helpless body. The doctors had tried everything they knew to do, even sedation, which did not seem to even affect the violent spasms.

As I was listening to my friend tell me of this poor little one, tears filled my eyes as I remember the complete sense of loss of control and despair when my own son had a fever of 105 when he was only several years old. He, too, had convulsions and the fever went to 106. The panic that a parent feels at such a time is inexplicable.

My friend continued after my interruption, saying, "Then you can imagine how these parents must have felt as they looked over their child in the hospital bed, but they were both *doctors*! Think of how they felt as *both* parent and doctor!"

Some time before this, Martha had read about a minister's wife who was said to have been blessed with an ability to heal. There were many stories about people who were more or less considered ''beyond the help of modern medicine" who had turned to her for help. She and her husband had a weekly healing service in their church. Martha turned to her husband tearfully, saying: "We're losing her, honey, I can't stand it anymore . . . there is nothing else we can do! I'm going to call the Reverend Mitchell's wife."

Martha barely had the words out of her mouth when the phone in her hand and the number she had dialed responded to her. "Yes, can I help you?" she heard in the receiver. "Oh, I hope so," cried Martha. "You don't know me, but, oh, I don't even know where to begin. Our little girl is dying, she's dying. Please, please, can you help us? I have heard about you and read about your gift of healing . . . please help us." Mrs. Williamson could hardly get the words out through her grieving and anxious tears. "Can you heal our daughter?"

Mrs. Mitchell had a calm and loving voice that responded to Martha's plea by saying, "Only God can heal, dear, only God. But if it is God's will, maybe God can use me to help you. I need to know a few things. Tell me right now where you are and where is your little girl?"

Martha told her that both she and her husband stood by the child's side as they spoke. "I am using the phone next to her hospital bed, and my husband is here with me," she said.

Martha's attention was drawn away from the phone. Her daughter was convulsing again. Jenny's seizures were occurring every three to four minutes, and a nurse had just entered the room to give her another shot to attempt to slow the convulsions.

Mrs. Mitchell said to Martha, "I need you to listen to me. I need you to *pray* for your daughter's recovery with me."

Panic-stricken by the suffering of her daughter, Martha blurted out, "Help us. We can't lose her. Our Jenny . . . oh, no." She lost control of her emotions, handing the phone to her husband.

"This is Dr. Williamson, Mrs. Mitchell. I'm sorry to bother you like this, but whatever help you can give us right now, we would sure appreciate it!"

Mrs. Mitchell responded by saying, "No trouble. Are you a Ph.D. doctor or a medical doctor, if you don't mind my asking?"

Dr. Williamson explained that he and his wife were medical doctors. "So, you are healers, too," she said back to him. Hearing that brought Dr. Williamson's emotions to the point where he, too, lost the tightly controlled state he had maintained. Tears began to run down his cheeks as he revealed that they do their best as doctors, always, "But we are not always successful. And now, with our little Jenny, well, we just don't know what else to do," he sobbed.

"I just told your wife that I need her to pray with me for your Jenny. I need you to pray for her, too. Do you believe in the power of prayer, Doctor?"

Looking at his precious daughter burning with

fever, convulsing, and near death, he said with anguish, "I don't really know for sure . . . I guess I do. I'm not certain," he stammered, "I suppose I have believed more in science and in orthodox medicine . . . until now. We have done all we possibly can . . . and it isn't helping," he lamented.

"Okay," Mrs. Mitchell said, "there is nothing really wrong with that, as long as you don't leave God out of the whole process of healing. God works through medicine, too—and science. Do you believe that?" she continued.

"Yes, yes, I do," the doctor answered. But deep within he wondered if she could read his subconscious feelings surfacing. He was thinking that in reality, he would probably have scoffed at the very idea of calling a Methodist minister and his wife with any question other than what is your sermon going to be this Sunday, but certainly, he as a medical doctor would not be calling to ask for physical healing for his only daughter! He found himself caught between the irony of feeling "what can she possibly do to help?" and the sense of complete despair and desperation of "please help, *please* help!"

As though she were sensing the doctor's faith (at least, former faith) in science, the healer said, "What we are about to do *is* science! Prayer is scientific. Prayer is 'soul' science, Doctor, prayer is soul science. If God wills it, you will see that it works!

"Now, if you still want my help, I need to tell you that I will need to do a little preparation," Mrs.

Mitchell said. Acknowledging his yes response, she continued, "I need to quiet myself for a little bit. Then, I will begin to pray very intensely for Jenny at precisely eight-thirty—that is only about a half hour away. At exactly that time, I ask you and your wife to place your right hands on your little girl's forehead and pray. I will be praying for her from here at the same time. Do you understand?"

"Yes, we do," he said while looking at his wife who was close enough to the phone to hear, or at least be able to piece the conversation together, he surmised, because she was nodding profusely in eager agreement to do anything that might help. What did they have to lose in trying? they thought.

The anxious couple sat down in chairs they had pushed together by Jenny's bedside. Holding hands, they both shed more tears, but did not speak. Each of them sat with the clock in the hall (outside the hospital room door) enough in view through the crack in the partly open door to gaze on it frequently, wishing the time would hurry up and be 8:30. Knowing that there was not time to spare for their little girl's sake, as every minute held the delicate balance of their Jenny's entire life.

Martha was called back in her mind to a time when she did feel that she had faith in God. She had been raised more conventionally religious than her husband. But somehow, somewhere along the line, in med. school and the years that followed, it just slipped into a lesser place. In fact, it just didn't seem to come up much in the busy lives they led.

Fred Williamson was asking himself silently, when was the last time he really felt a belief in God? He knew he used to, but he was all too acutely aware now, that he didn't even think about it, and hadn't for a very long time. He became aware of "snippets" of memory pictures that floated through his mind. Some of them so real that it took him back in time to when he served his four years as an army doctor. The terrible destruction, maiming, and suffering that he experienced during that time fleeted through his mind like an old war movie. He shook, as if to shake those terrible thoughts and pictures out of his head, when he noticed the clock. It was now 8:25.

He turned and looked at his wife, who noticed that he had broken out in a sweat. Asking him if he was okay, she brought him back to the present and they squeezed each other's hands very tight, then hugged. At that moment it almost seemed that each of them was tuned into what the other had been thinking during that short time that seemed like a near eternity. They felt an exceptional oneness of purpose and desire with the clock approaching 8:30.

The couple rose from their chairs and made their way to the hospital bed, where their daughter was experiencing another of the seizures. At precisely 8:30 they both (one on each side of the bed) laid their right hands on Jenny's head. Both of them struggled with trepidation and fear for the first few seconds they touched their daughter, as they were reminded of the scorching fever that ravaged her little body.

Fred and Martha looked at each other (hands still on Jenny's forehead), recognizing that they were both ready to pray. It was as though the fear instantly melted away in each other's glance, and hope took its place. Their prayer was barely finished with "Please help us, God, heal our Jenny, Oh Lord, please hear our prayer" when to their astonishment, Jenny let out a sigh and she fell into a relaxed and natural sleep from the comalike state she had been in.

The attending nurse happened to be in the room at the time of the prayer. She had been there through much of the early evening, although she would give the Williamsons privacy when she sensed it was appropriate. She burst out saying, "Look, her seizures stopped. I noticed that they stopped the minute you two put your hands on her head." She explained how at first she thought that was just coincidence, but then they did not start up again!

And that is just what the nurse entered in her patient report. "From the moment Jenny's parents placed their hands on her forehead, she began to give visible signs of relaxing. The convulsive seizures that I had been unsuccessfully treating for hours—stopped. She suffered no additional seizures."

As doctors, of course, the parents knew the best sign they could have was the lapsing into a natural sleep state and the cessation of the tremors. She was not out of danger yet, but there had definitely been a "break" in her condition—at the exact time of the prayer.

Martha and Fred hugged each other like they hadn't in a long time! Almost at once they all (joined by the nurse) shouted out thank you, God! Martha immediately went to the phone, calling Mrs. Mitchell to report what had happened. "Please . . . KEEP praying!" she pleaded.

Throughout the night, Mom and Dad maintained a vigil at the bedside of their sleeping daughter. Dozing in and out of sleep, as much as this is possible in a chair, by morning when Martha opened her eyes, she noticed that her daughter's side was no longer paralyzed! By afternoon she had improved so dramatically that they could all actually see "life" in her body again. It was as though they had actually witnessed their daughter going from frightfully close to death—to life, in less than twenty-four hours!

Three days later, Mrs. Mitchell came to the hospital to visit Jenny and to meet her parents. None of them had ever met before, yet the minute Mrs. Mitchell walked into Jenny's room a very strange thing happened.

Little Jenny took one look at Mrs. Mitchell, not knowing who this visitor was, and excitedly announced to her mom and dad, "That's the nice lady who visited me in heaven!"

Utterly mesmerized, the Williamsons invited their daughter to tell them more, as Mrs. Mitchell just smiled and listened attentively.

"Two beautiful angels were walking with me and a bunch of other children in heaven," Jenny said. "At first I was sad to leave Mommy and Daddy, but the angels were so kind and good to me and they said that my new home would be with them in heaven. Then this nice lady came walking up to the angels and told them that they would have to let me go back. She told them that my mommy and daddy needed me so much that I must go right back with her."

Both Fred and Martha began to weep. Martha walked over to Jenny and held her hand tightly, saying, "This nice lady was right, sweetheart, your mommy and daddy couldn't live without you."

Not surprised, but expressing a very open attitude about what Jenny had described, Mrs. Mitchell said to them all, "No one really knows what great energies are released when one really prays as intensely as I was, and as your mommy and daddy were," she added, as she looked at Jenny and winked. "Who knows? Maybe some part of my psyche or consciousness *did* go to heaven to plead Jenny's case before the angels. We never know the mystery and wonder of the miracle workings of God!"

A mere ten days after that remarkable demonstration of the power of prayer to bring healing to a very sick little eight-year-old girl, Jenny was released from the hospital and allowed to return home.

By Christmastime, two months later, Jenny had all her energy and health back. She was now officially cured and celebrated a very joyous Christmas with two very grateful parents. The Doctors Williamson, were thankful not only for a miracle healing, but for their own renewed faith, and their definitely expanded skills and beliefs in healing to include *prayer*!

10

Prayer Spares Me from a Surgeon's Knife

"It just can't be! NO! It'll be gone any second now, oh my God!" Silent thoughts to my children and husband, but to me they were denying the sheer panic by screaming in my head. I had just served the last dish at the dinner table—my family's favorite—mashed potatoes, all steamy and punctuated with butter melting down the sides like snow down a mountain.

Maybe that is what the added thoughts of disbelief were triggered by . . . "I am healthy as can be! I'm always the last one down the ski slopes, and even then I try to get in just one more run before the resort closes for the night." Mentally I was seeing myself skiing down the mountain just as I had been the very last week. It was so clear and realistic that for a fraction of a second I forgot where I was. It seemed as though I *was* skiing!

Suddenly I became aware of my husband yelling my name. Erik blurted out, "Mommy, what's wrong?" Then I became aware that I must have blacked out, and when I came to, I was clutching at my chest. Now Melissa was getting worried. Too young to know what was happening, she must have been responding to the panic in the air.

I don't remember what happened next until I was in the hospital emergency room, looking up at many white coats looking down at me! "Where am I? What's going on?" Of course the answers I received didn't make sense to me at all! "Can you tell us what happened? Do you remember? Have you had heart pains recently? Numbness anywhere, or a feeling of tightness?" The doctor and nurses were grilling me as though something very serious had happened and might happen again.

Confused, I said that I was okay now, but asked *them* what happened. My husband came in view as he recounted the final serving for the dinner meal that triggered this mess I was in. He explained that it seemed as if I blacked out, and had been clutching my chest, saying, "Oh no . . . it cannot be!" Then an ambulance and emergency intervention.

It seems the doctor had already called in the cardiologist on call, then several more specialists were brought in to examine me. I could hardly believe it. I thought I was fine and ready to return home, still not understanding what had happened. I must have still been in some kind of a "state."

Remembering that many questions had been asked about my heart, I said to one of the specialists (as he was listening to my chest), and even though he *didn't* ask, "my heart has been just fine. I have not had any problems at all that I'm aware of since I had rheumatic fever when I was a child." He didn't seem to pay much attention to what I'd said, but was more intent on listening and listening again at different points on my chest and back.

I'd been hooked up for a few tests and felt like a guinea pig on a gurney the way everyone was poking and listening. Then it came, "You seem to have suffered some kind of attack here with your heart, my dear, has this ever happened before?"

Doesn't anybody here listen! (I was too polite to say that out loud, but that is definitely what I was thinking!) I reminded them that I said that I was not aware of any heart incident or problems or "signs." Telling them that I was extremely busy and very, very active and *never*, ever blacked out before (since that, too, was the consensus, that I had blacked out).

Then it was sixty questions about the rheumatic fever particulars. When I was about five years old, I did almost die with it. It was fortunate that it was caught in time and although I was completely bedridden for all of first grade, I survived. At the end of the year when I was able to get up, I still had to have penicillin shots once a week for what seemed like years.

I had been left with a heart murmur that would

not allow me to do the fun playground things in school, once I was able to start back at second grade. No running, swinging, or relay games allowed for quite a few years. Then about sixth grade it seemed the murmur had cleared up enough that I could start moderate activities. Finally, in high school, I think it had disappeared. From that time on I was a whirlwind of activity! "So, I must be fine now," I said. "Maybe I have the flu or something and just got dizzy," I tried to convince them.

Then someone dropped the bomb! "As you know, we told you we wanted several opinions. We now have all conferred (referring to the other doctors who had been called in), are in agreement. If we don't operate on you right away, you will be dead in twenty-four hours."

There was no way I could be hearing right! "What?" I gasped! The doctor continued, "You have a hole in your heart that sounds very, very bad. It is posing an immediate danger. If we don't do open heart surgery on you as soon as possible, you will bleed to death internally." They were definitive. There was no question in any of their minds. Because I was conscious, I needed to give my approval.

How could I possibly do that? Everything I was hearing and seeing around me now became so surrealistic. It was as though I'd been thrust in the middle of a dramatic film as the leading star abut to be sliced open. I'd never watched a soap opera, but now, I was it! Thoughts came back to me of many things

I'd witnessed in nurses' training. Judgmental, perhaps, but I was convinced that at least one-half of the surgeries were not necessary (well, maybe not one half, but a lot!).

Then it hit me again, as one of the doctors said, "There isn't much time, you have a beautiful family, you are young and vital. You have a lot to live for!" That they were talking to and about me!

"No," I told them, "there must be a mistake. It is impossible that I have a hole that fast! Why wouldn't I have had some warning of heart problems, other signs, gradually? This doesn't make any sense to go from no problems to open heart surgery in a matter of minutes!" On and on I went, basically in complete and total disbelief.

The doctors were getting a bit impatient probably, as they continued to explain the seriousness and the urgency of the matter. What got into me, I really don't know, except that it be the conviction of the Holy Spirit that I did not need surgery! This could be dangerous—thinking one knows better than top specialists and medical experts—I was thinking, and my husband promptly reminded me.

I am, and always have been, "a stubborn Swede," so I've been told (and I confess, it's true—*once in a while*). It was as though every ounce of me simply knew better. Right, I'm smarter than all these doctors!

Knowing that denial and shock is very normal, and that I seemed to be quite *in* both, the doctors were very patient with me. I asked if I could have a few moments alone, to pray about it. They all seemed hesitant, as time seemed to be of the essence, but they granted my wish (hopefully, not my dying request).

So, I prayed. I prayed real hard. I asked God for help and to show me if I was wrong. I really did feel that God works through the miracle and blessing of skilled doctors and surgeons, as well as through miracles of the Divine and supernatural nature; so it wasn't as though I was terrified of surgery, or did not believe in doctors. My turning deep within and completely to God gave me an immediate answer. "NO!"

That is what I heard. It was loud and clear and it felt solid. "No, you don't *need* surgery," I was told. When I get a certain feeling from a depth without question, I have learned in the past that I'd better follow it. It has always been right.

When I shared the results of my prayer time and consequently the decision I made with my husband and the doctors, the resulting horror on their faces and their attempts to dissuade me seem duly recorded in some canvas-like recess of my mind. At first, it seemed as if they thought I must have a death wish, but then they allowed my insisted compromise.

I decided to be checked into the hospital and requested more extensive tests. I felt no fear. I was not scared that I might be wrong, or that it was just a "hopeful" voice in my head that was more reflecting what *I* wanted to hear, rather than actually being God's answer to me for my urgent request, in prayer.

"You have such beautiful children." "What a darling little redhead Erik is . . ." "I bet they call him Erik the Red!" "And Melissa . . . she is adorable!" "You are sooo lucky!" Almost as if they were trying to talk some sense into me, the nurses were just doing what they thought best. But nothing changed my mind.

I guess the first sign that God was right was that twenty-four hours later, I was still alive! As it turned out, the results of every test administered came back as a complete surprise to the medical staff.

Yes, there was a hole. It was in a valve from my heart. However, the shocking news was the *size* of the hole. Although it was right where the diagnosis predicted, it was small. It did not pose an immediate life or death threat. No surgery was needed!

The explanation to me was that for some odd reason, the *sound* that was audible for a "leaky valve" in the examination and listening process somehow was greatly amplified within my chest. Something was acting as an acoustic amplifier, making the hole sound much much larger than it was in reality. This is why the judgment of all concerned was for immediate surgery. That truly was the safest and the correct prognosis for the situation.

It was explained that I would have to be extremely cautious, as they told me how I could safely live to even be a fairly ripe old age, as long as I took certain precautions, and was reasonably mindful of my condition. That felt more like it, I thought, yet I was still slightly surprised that there was *any* hole at all!

But, I decided, I was certainly grateful to have "a leaky valve" even though it made me sound like an old '48 Chevy or something, rather than a chest full of stitches. I gave thanks and praise to God!

I can't quite recall just how many people asked me how I knew, and where did I get such a strong and stubborn conviction that I did not need surgery, even though all the doctors said I did. My husband couldn't resist the "stubborn Swede" comment, but I laughed at that, then said, "Well, maybe just a little of that, too, but mainly it was the power of prayer!"

How Do You Really Know?

I want to make it clear that I am not advocating that anyone who disagrees with a diagnosis from a physician or surgeon follow their inner voice if that voice tells them to do different. It is not automatic that what might seem like an answer one hears inside one's head is always the right voice. Discerning between one's own thoughts, or even strange thoughts from elsewhere, can be a very complex matter.

So, just how can we be certain we are hearing or getting a genuine answer to prayer and not just wishful thinking on our own behalf? How does one really *know*?

~ 11 ~

Absent Healing

Absent healing sounds somewhat like a contradiction in terms, doesn't it? I mean, how are you going to be healed if you aren't there! What the term really means is the person who may not be able to attend a church service, a healing service, a prayer group or session is healed—from a distance.

A regular member of *Prayer Heals Double Fracture*, my weekly prayer group, was not there one evening. As we were gathering and getting ready to start our group session, the phone rang. It was Judy's husband calling to say there had been an accident and Judy was not going to be able to make it that night.

He proceeded to explain that he was calling from the emergency room in the hospital. Karl and his wife had been roller-skating at a large roller rink, having a wonderful time skating to music in a family outing with their kids. Karl said that some little kid weaved right in front of Judy, causing her to fall. I loved to skate with my kids, too, and I could just visualize the whole scene.

Karl said that Judy was in extreme agony. She could be heard moaning in the background. "Honey, this is ridiculous," he said to her, "come on now, *please* let the doctor take care of it!" He said it almost like he forgot he was on the phone. Judy was coaching him between her painful groans to just please do what she said.

Judy did not want Karl to tell us what happened to her. The details of her accident (other than that she fell) were not to be revealed to us. Her request was that someone sit in for healing for her, in her place, in our healing circle when we got to that part of our session. "She is saying to see if anyone in the prayer group 'picks up' on what her injury is," Karl relayed.

"Oh, c-o-m-e o-n Judy, give me a break; this isn't a game!" Karl did not quite relate, as maybe most caring husbands wouldn't, when their loved one was suffering greatly, but would not let the doctor "fix" her, yet she was willing to go to the hospital to check it out! "What gives, Judy, I do not understand you!" Karl added.

Karl politely said, "Excuse me just a minute, I'm sorry, just a minute, don't go away—I'll be back in a minute!" At that point, he covered the phone with his hand, muffling the sounds of their conversation. "Okay, I guess it doesn't matter what I think! Judy says this prayer group is documenting the power of prayer and healing and that she is willing and WANTING to be prayed for—first. She had X-rays taken, but she refuses to let them touch her. As you already know, she doesn't want me to tell you what's wrong. She wants me to take her home now so she can be in bed at the time you all pray. She will pray with you at that exact time." Karl had dutifully carried out the message that was shared with the rest of the group immediately.

We followed the service format, and once again (as had happened several times before) the discussion of the spiritual reading of scripture and the personal application and questions lasted quite a bit beyond the time we tried to stick to for the "group prayer circle" where we placed special emphasis on praying for "healing."

We tried to keep an approximate time, both for reasons of holding the service to a few hours, and to give those who had asked us for prayers and those who could not come a time to synchronize around. Then they would join in, praying from wherever they were. As a group we had agreed that *if* the discussion was unusually personal and called for more time, that we would give that time, rather than be "institutional" with a regimented allotted time. There are more reasons than not why keeping to a schedule—for church, or any meeting is important, but we all felt that true growth—spiritually, required more than that type of service could allow for.

Someone in our group glanced at her watch and blurted out with surprise, "Oh, my, it is already nine thirty-five! We have gone w-a-y over!" There were a few who had to hurry and leave because of a baby-sitter or some other reason, while the rest of us gathered in a circle. We joined hands, took several long, slow, deep breaths to relax and let go of all that the day and the group discussion had brought us, and to just ready ourselves for prayer.

We recited the 23rd Psalm together first, then we said the Lord's Prayer in unison. I volunteered to sit in the middle and be Judy's proxy. The rest of the group would lay hands on my head as I said a prayer for Judy, then silently all would say a prayer, and if anyone wanted to add anything out loud, they were free to do so. There is a distinct energy that can be felt, when the prayer is done. At times the feeling is very palpable. It can be very electric.

At one point, I saw a very clear image of an arm with a double fracture; others said they saw that, too. At the time, it seems we even were able to distinguish which arm (left or right). We prayed again, then someone else requested to sit in for another request. Then one at a time we went around the circle for each one of our prayer requests, individually ours, or given to us by someone else. Then we sat for an additional moment of silence, then we usually had some coffee, tea, and cookies before we departed for home.

The phone rang. It was now about 10:45 P.M. It was Judy. She described with exuberance just what had happened to her on the other end. She said the pain was so severe that she almost didn't make it. She had Karl help her get ready for bed and climbed under the covers. Karl turned on the television at the foot of their bed and tuned into a program that caught his interest. Judy said she kept watching the clock and gritting her teeth, not sure if she could hold out.

"Karl got really mad at me," she said, "I mean, it got to the point where he was just about screaming at me that he was just going to physically carry me to the car and take me back to the hospital. 'Enough is enough,'" she said he yelled, continuing, "'This is completely absurd, Judy, that's it—we're going! You know God heals through doctors, too! What in the world is wrong with that? You are just being stubborn, but *I* can't take your pain anymore!'"

Judy said she didn't blame him, because as the time for our prayer circle came and went, she prayed, then she asked Karl to please pray with her, too. "Nothing happened!" she said. "I don't really know what I expected, but when the pain wasn't even a little better, but in fact, got worse, I almost decided to let him take me back to the hospital."

She went on to describe her agony of holding out "just one more hour. By that time, Karl wasn't even talking to me. At nine-thirty, I looked straight at the clock again, as I thought about what Karl had said earlier, about God working through doctors, too. I was thinking maybe he was right, maybe I was being stubborn. I was just about to say, okay, you're probably right, honey, let's go back to the emergency room. They'll probably think I am crazy but, what else is new! When I felt like somebody had dropped a bag of hot coals on my feet! I let out a scream, and yelled for Karl.

" 'Oh, my God, Karl, do you feel something hot like fire under the covers? Do you have a heating pad or something?' " He looked at her strangely, she said, then described how suddenly the heat became a distinct "ring of fire." She said it was almost like a Hula-Hoop of extreme heat. It continued to move up her legs very slowly. "When it got to the middle of my body and then to my arms, the pain was gone! It was unbelievable! It continued to move over my body and head to the very top, then it slowly moved back down. At any point in the whole process, I could have pointed to exactly 'where' it was! When the ring of fire left my feet, I knew I was healed! My arm was healed!"

The group had gathered around the phone, as they sensed that something incredible was being shared. The air was electric as we all squealed and shouted for joy, and we were almost stunned that we had all picked up on the right body part that had been hurt!

When we were told the details of the accident, the

trip to the hospital, and that the X-rays confirmed a compound fracture that needed setting and a cast immediately, we began to have it really sink in what a true miracle it was. "Judy, are you sure?" "I am sure! I can move my arm without pain—even."

Somehow, we didn't feel very comfortable about her decision. Maybe we even had a little doubt, and wanted just to be safe and certain that Judy was all right. We strongly suggested that she go back to the hospital anyway "Just to be sure." Judy said she was really tired, and she did not want to drag the kids out of bed, when they were sound asleep; so, she promised that she would go back to the hospital the next day "Just to be sure." We could all hear Karl in the background. "You can believe she will; I'll make sure of that!"

The next afternoon and evening, calls circulated from Judy to the group members, who in turn passed it on to one another. Judy had another dramatic addition to her miracle. When she and Karl arrived at the hospital, there was a different crew on staff. They examined her arm. She said, "They really gave me weird looks!" "Why do you think you have a broken arm, miss?" they had asked her.

Judy said both she and Karl explained the story several times before it sunk in with anyone. Finally, someone said, "You mean to tell me we have X-rays here from last night of your arm and they showed you arm to be broken—in two places?"

"It was almost a whole comedy routine!" Judy said,

laughing. "They really didn't believe me! Karl and I sat while they went to look for the proper files and the X-rays. They came back in the examining room." Judy said both the doctor and two nurses looked at the breaks in the arm on the negatives and shook their heads. "There must be a mistake here. Maybe someone else's X-rays got mixed up with yours."

"No way," Judy piped up. "That was MY pain! I guarantee you that; that was my pain all right—ask my husband!" Karl was eager to throw in his complaints at her seeming stubbornness the night before. Judy said that they left the room to go investigate the possibility that the records had been mixed up—by accident.

They came back to report that there wasn't anyone else that night with a double fracture on that same arm, so it could not have been someone else's broken arm. Then they were talking about strange things that occur occasionally, where the pain is so great that the body and brain block it out—temporarily— then it can come back and hit you with a vengeance, especially if you use it.

Not saying a thing, Judy cooperated with their ordering more X-rays "Just to be sure." And guess what?" she said, "they came back negative, not a trace of a break, much less two! PRAYER healed my arm!" She and her husband left the hospital with everyone "scratching their heads. I don't think they knew what to make of it all!" Judy said. "Everyone except Karl and me. Karl was there, he saw it for himself, with his own eyes. Now he believes!"

12

Prayer Locates Missing Body

⁓

Keep the faith: In every hurt or sorrow there
is an opportunity to Grow!

⁓

John and Charlotte Huser have had their share of
troubles and setbacks to deal with, some much
tougher than others; but what sets the Husers apart
is how they respond to them. They have an extremely
close-knit family, revolving around the many activities of the children. There is never a dull moment.
Yet the kind of people they are, they always find
time, no matter how busy they were, to help others.
Even though the demands on any family these days,
with the many responsibilities and pressures of life,
can be quite enough with one's own children, Charlotte and John always found room for one more.

Active in their church, school, and community, the Husers decided to broaden their perimeters even further—across the ocean and to different cultures. Eager to share their joy and love, they have been hosts to several foreign-exchange students over the years.

One of their former students, Petra, from Germany, missed her "American family" very much. Suggesting that they come visit her, she pleaded for them to come to Germany. Petra had a vacation coming up from her schooling in October, which she said was a perfect time of year to go to Germany. Besides, she said, "My family is eager to have you come here too!"

Now, for some time John Huser had been experiencing extreme pain in his joints. He had been able to cope with it by undergoing various treatments, and because of his strong faith; but progressively the pain worsened and became more and more disabling. His doctor recommended surgery for joint replacement. In August 1989 John had undergone one of many such surgeries. So even though the invitation to Germany was tempting, it seemed too soon after surgery to be possible.

In a moment of enthusiasm about this exciting invitation, they casually mentioned the possibility of a trip to Germany to John's doctor when they went for one of the post-surgery check-ups.

"That's wonderful," the doctor said. "How beautiful the autumn in Germany would be, and what a thrilling time of the year to go, with Octoberfests and colorful hillsides in festive fall colors. I can almost hear the sounds of oom-pa-pa oom-pa-pa bands and the smell of 'brats' on the grill."

When John and Charlotte got home, they began to reminisce about the excitement and smells of autumn—like going back to school, football games, and Halloween fun. They reflected on the many good times they'd had together. Then they remembered the different exchange students and some of the funnier incidents that came up during the process of getting to know and understand each other's cultural differences and customs. They were laughing so hard that tears were running down their cheeks.

"Think of what it would be like for us in another country. I bet we'd get some laughs," they both burst out saying at nearly the same time. Then the German trip offer came up, and they discussed how exciting it would be to go.

"Why don't you go?" Glen asked. "Really Mom and Dad, what better time than in October . . . The fact that Petra's family owns a ski resort doesn't hurt anything either, not that you'll be skiing down those slopes, or anything, Dad, but you two really do deserve a vacation. It really is about time!"

John and Charlotte filled their son in on what the doctor said; then Charlotte said with a motherly tone, "Oh, this is all great fun, but we all know it is just a bit out of our capability right now. I mean, really,

Glen, you know how expensive first-class tickets would be . . . why, we can't even think of it!"

"But it sure is fun pretending," John added.

Glen, with a somewhat pensive expression, asked, "No, really, just say you *had* the tickets. If the ticket expense were not the consideration here, would you go?" Their response was immediate. "Of course we would," they both laughed and said together, "We'd *love* to go!"

"That was all that was said. It never even crossed our minds that Glen might have had something in mind," Charlotte told me. "Never in our wildest dreams would we have guessed that Glen was going to make this possible for us," she continued.

"Later that month, he unveiled his surprise to us. It would be my birthday on October 10, and Glen said, 'This is something I *really* want to do for you guys.' I couldn't believe it—we were really going to Germany!"

As Charlotte continued to relate the story to me, it was as if I could feel the excitement myself for what just such a surprise gift would do to me. The elation, the preparations, the packing and making certain that everything was taken care of on the home front while they were gone, and, of course, being sure that the doctor's and other important phone numbers were along.

As if all this wasn't exciting enough, the Husers were told by friends that they too would be in Germany around the 18th of October. Having written a musical that was to be presented in Oberammergau, Germany, they immediately mentioned the possibility of the Husers joining them for the big day. As they continued to marvel at the awesome coincidence of both families being in Germany at that time, an idea occurred to their friends. Not only were they invited to attend, they were invited to sing in the chorale which would be led by some of the musicians of the famed evangelist, Billy Graham!

The time for the trip was at hand. Everything was more than wonderful. The trip to visit their German daughter, Petra, was all but perfect. They'd had a marvelous time with Petra and her parents at the enchanting ski resort they owned. What could possibly top this!

The memorable trip, of course, was to be capped with the grand musical that they were to be a part of! So off they went with the arrangements they had made to travel from Petra's to Oberammergau. Upon arriving at their hotel, they emptied their luggage, settling into their room.

When they returned to the hotel after dinner, the manager saw them and told them there was an extremely urgent message for them. He told them the police were trying to locate them to tell them to "call home." Not knowing what the message could possibly be, one can only imagine the dread they felt at such a time.

The news was not good. They were told that their son Glen had been killed in a parasailing accident in

Tulsa, Oklahoma. He had died Saturday afternoon, October 14th.

Hearing such words brought a tornado of emotions. "It can't be true . . . it simply can not be . . . we must be dreaming . . . they have the wrong person . . . no . . . NO! Not our Glen . . . NO."

"We immediately called for a taxi to go to Munich. We had to get back. We had to get on an airplane as soon as possible," Charlotte told me. "We arrived at the Munich airport at midnight and sat there all night long." They would have to wait until the employees arrived for the new day of ticketing passengers.

With emotions completely raw and yet numb at the same time, the Husers witnessed the gradual hum of activity begin to build as the airport staff arrived, getting ready for the coming and going of passengers.

Trying to take care of changing your tickets for a different departure time is a strange and awkward thing at such a time. It has to be done, but sometimes it is hard to form the right words without being overcome by the pain of the news that made this task necessary.

Procedures, rules and regulations often add more confusion and turmoil than imaginable at delicate times like this. But, Charlotte told me that American Airlines were very kind. Without any ado, they sympathetically helped to make the process go as smoothly as possible, providing the Husers with first-class tickets to the United States.

After settling into their seats, the Husers breathed a deep sigh of relief that they made the flight and were on their way. In the hustle of what had to be done to get to this point, there were moments when it seemed they weren't even sure just where they were going, or, why! Suddenly, it hit them again that they were on their way home—they were going home, but not at all in the way it had been planned. This was hardly the grand finale they were to have to this incredible trip to Germany—their gift from Glen. They once again felt the stabbing dagger sensation in their chest, and the tears swelled once again. They sat together in a stupor—not really knowing what was ahead and quickly forgetting the beauty of what had gone before.

Not completely aware of how much time had passed, Charlotte said she wasn't really even thinking, she just was in an almost meditative state, when she heard someone talk to her. She knew it wasn't her husband. The voice said to her: "Mom, I'm all right." Then again, even more emphatically, "Mom, I'm *all right!*" There was no disputing that it *was* Glen's voice. It was as though her son was right there with her, talking to her in a manner sure to capture her attention!

Once she became acutely aware that Glen wasn't really there, she began to cry again. Getting out more tissues to wipe away her tears, she told her husband with great emotion what she had just experienced. Instead of making both of them feel worse, a kind of peace came upon them with Glen's reassuring words of comfort . . . *whatever* they meant.

When they arrived at the airport in Kansas City, Missouri, they were met by John's sister, and they returned to their home in southwest Missouri. It was extremely late by the time they pulled into their driveway. It was 4 a.m., and they were completely exhausted and emotionally drained. It didn't help matters to know that they had to prepare to leave early that very day, for a trip to Tulsa, Oklahoma.

After very little rest they left to meet with the Oklahoma Water Patrol. They were to be taken out by boat on Keystone Lake and would be shown just where their son's accident had occurred. But, there was more bad news. After many attempts, they had not been able to locate the body.

The Husers continued to travel back and forth many times over the next three months, hoping to find their son's body; but it was not to be found.

Charlotte Huser was understandably having a very difficult time sleeping at night. She used that time to read and study the Bible, seeking further strength and guidance to make sense of their devastating loss. She told me that on the 53rd day, something happened that in and of itself was a remarkable coincidence.

At 4 a.m., she turned on the television and a Brother Mack Lyon from Edmund Oklahoma Church of Christ was preaching a sermon on "Dealing with Grief." Knowing that was exactly what she needed, she settled back and listened with great interest. Brother Mack had announced that anyone could call his church if they had any special requests. Charlotte felt a strong need at that moment to have someone pray with and for their situation.

It suddenly dawned on Charlotte that she had not prayed even once for her son's body to be found. This oversight hardly seemed possible, so she called the church of Brother Mack Lyon, asking them to pray for Glen's body to be finally located. Feeling a strong surge of another request, she asked for prayers to keep those who were searching the waters for the body safe.

That same afternoon, her husband came home reporting that a Tulsa radio station had reported the drowning of a fireman. He had a very funny feeling about it. Then, suddenly their telephone rang. It was a call from the Oklahoma Water Patrol saying that their son's body had been found by a fireman scuba diving.

Quickly, they turned on the radio, tuning in to a station that they thought might be able to pick up more details as they became available.

Finding out the name of the hospital where the fireman had been taken, Charlotte called to talk with him, if possible. She was told the terrible news that the fireman did not make it. The hospital gave her the name of the fireman, but they were not allowed to give out any more information.

The Husers then called the Fire Department in the

hopes of getting the fireman's family's telephone number. They were told that out of consideration for the family they could not give out the number. Charlotte was not satisfied by this, however—she felt strongly that she needed to talk to the family of the man who lost his life in order to find their son.

Something told her to call Brother Mack Lyon again for his help. Not knowing this when she called, it turned out that his church was in the very same town where the fireman lived! Brother Mack Lyon called the Husers back to personally express his sympathy and to give them the telephone number of the fireman's family.

A very deep pain was felt in the pit of Charlotte's stomach when she called the number to hear an answering machine message with the voice of that very same fireman.

Charlotte called quite a few times before getting an actual person instead of the answering machine. She was able to talk with family members and to express how thankful they were that their son's body had been found *in answer to* prayer that very day. It was hard to bear, however, that an act of kindness should bring about the death of such a heroic man. The families could understand each other's grief, and later became friends.

I find something else truly remarkable about the Husers. They have accepted that there are many things that we do not know. Such a sad occurrence did not diminish their faith in God. They remained grateful that their prayers to locate the body of their beloved son had been answered within hours.

Their faith could have been tarnished and their belief in God diminished at the loss of their son and the death of his rescuer—a double tragedy. Not only did they refuse to allow this to occur, they turned their loss into glorifying God. They continued to pray so that they may call upon God and their faith in order to help others.

⁓

> Do not pray for easy lives. Pray to be stronger men. Do not pray for tasks equal to your powers. Pray for powers equal to your tasks. Then the doing of your work shall be no miracle, but *you* shall be the miracle.—PHILLIPS BROOKS

13

Prayer Heals a Dangerously High Fever—Instantly

It was noticeable at the dinner table that my son Erik was not feeling his normal rambunctious self. Not only was he not interested in eating the meal set before him, he wasn't even tempted by his favorite dessert! Noticing that his face was a bit flushed, I asked him if he wanted to go lie down on the couch in the family room.

Before Erik could answer, his younger sister Melissa blurted out from her high chair, "I do, Mommy, me too!" Smiling at her eagerness to get back to playing with her brother and their toys, I reminded her to finish her dinner—if she wanted dessert; and that Erik didn't feel very good, so he wouldn't be playing with her. That appeased her into bringing her attention back around to eating, while Erik quietly slipped out of his chair and went to the couch.

Before I cleared the table of the dinner dishes, I went to check on Erik. Finding him asleep, I covered him with a blanket. His forehead felt *very* warm, so I expressed my concern to his dad. I had a prayer group that evening that I would soon need to be getting ready for; and it wasn't very long before I would have to leave. Erik's dad said not to worry, he would keep a close watch on him and keep checking on his fever.

Hurriedly, I went about the task of clearing the dining-room table. The entire time I was working in the kitchen that "motherly instinct" of worry for her child kept building up in me. When I had the last dish put away and the table wiped, I rushed out to feel Erik's forehead again.

Shocked that he felt warmer still to the touch than the very last time I had checked, I blurted out, "Oh my God, he feels much hotter now." I got out the thermometer, took his temperature (which had elevated to slightly over 101), then stated rather matter-of-factly: "I'd better call the doctor and not go to the prayer group."

Stopping me in my tracks and panic, my husband calmly said, "No, he will be okay! You *go* to the prayer group and *pray* for Erik's fever!"

I must confess that my reaction to such a comment was not good! Inside I was thinking, pray for him? What Erik needs is a house call by the doctor—*Now!*

Somehow, such a declaration of faith seemed more to me to be a lack of concern.

Precipitating in my mind were more terrifying "fear" thoughts bubbling up from within and overflowing. The pull of my love and concern for my only son was weighing on my consciousness as though it was my right and obligation as a mom to stay home and be sure that he was attended to, and if that meant calling a doctor, that's that!

This particular prayer group was especially important to me. My passion was in healing and what made it work for some and not others. Loving people, and seeing so many in need of miracles, I felt very dedicated to this prayer group and the emphasis that we as a group had placed on prayer and *healing*! It was almost a research interest in that aspect of prayer. I didn't think I doubted for a minute the efficacy of the power of prayer, and I wanted to "document" the occurrences of each member and the events as they unfolded.

All at once, I became even more aware of the struggle and pull within me between motherhood and a healing ministry. Acutely feeling the betrayal stirring in my heart and mind, I stood conflicted. I hadn't recalled ever being in a situation just like this one before. Never was I confronted in such a bold manner (that I could remember at that very moment, anyway) about my faith in the power of prayer.

At that precise confrontation, the sinking feeling hit me that I must not have a strong enough *belief* in the power of prayer alone to heal! When it came right down to it, and when it came this close to home, my belief seemed to be, "Pray, then call the doctor!" I became strangely confused.

Suddenly I felt nearly immobilized. I just couldn't leave my son that way! No way was I going to leave his side when he was nearly on fire with a fever. Of course, I wasn't going to leave town or be gone for more than a few hours or so; but what if he had something really serious, or he got worse? He would probably feel that his mom put the meeting first and didn't even care that he had a high fever and was ill! All these thoughts and many more battled on in my brain.

My husband was so firm about my going ahead with my commitment to the prayer group and that Erik would be fine, that as I fixed baby aspirin and managed to get it down Erik, I could feel the turmoil within me begin to ease. I knew the baby aspirin would soon take effect, and Daddy promised that he would call me immediately if there was the slightest change for the worse.

I hustled up to the bedroom to throw on some clothes. When I was ready to go, I reminded Daddy of the time we in the group had ordained for the purpose of dedicated healing, and asked that he join us in prayer at that time for Erik. Then I was off.

As things worked out, our normal healing circle time was altered by over an hour because of a long discussion, but when we got to it, I sat in for Erik. The group laid hands on me and prayed for his healing.

When I arrived home, my husband, who had been asleep on the couch, sprang up with tremendous excitement to share his story. It seemed that Erik's temperature had shot up to 104 degrees while I was gone. At first that brought his very concerned father near panic, but he managed to regain his composure and consoled himself with the thought that God would heal Erik through our prayer circle. In fact, he consoled himself so thoroughly that he fell asleep.

When he awakened, he looked at the clock and saw that he had slept through the time when he was to lay hands on Erik and he felt guilty. Erik, however, who had fallen asleep on the couch with him, got up and began to make his way up the stairs. Startled, Daddy awakened in time to see Erik climbing the stairs, whereupon he demanded that Erik come back and lie down. "It's all right, Daddy," Erik told him. "Mommy's prayer healed me. I'm all right now. I'm just going upstairs to get some toys."

Daddy took Erik's temperature and was astonished to see that it was normal.

When he was telling me that he felt so bad that he had fallen asleep and missed the time he was to lay hands on Erik, he mentioned that he did look at his watch when Erik told him he was healed. It was within just a few minutes of the time that the laying-on-of-hands prayer session began—which would have been exactly enough time for me to get seated in the middle of our group and begin praying for Erik!

～ 14 ～

Prayer and Spiritual Healing

Olga and Ambrose Worrall

The late Olga Worrall was not only one of the greatest healers of modern times, but she was one of the kindest and most giving women I have ever met. Her wide acclaim of praying for the "incurable" reached scientists at many major universities and institutions. Many wished to research her abilities. The Institutes of Health and Education were among those that conducted many experiments with her to see if there was any "measurable" effect in her healing that could be scientifically proven. It was through several of the scientists working with Olga that she and I were introduced.

Every Thursday morning for more than three decades, hundreds of sick people filled the Mount Washington Methodist Church in Baltimore, Maryland, to receive spiritual healing from this wonderful woman. At precisely nine o'clock every night those same supplicants, along with thousands of others across the world who had called or written seeking absent healing for physical and mental ailments, paused for five minutes to give and receive the healing energy that flowed into them from God through the focus of this gifted spiritual battery.

Olga and her husband Ambrose began their public ministry in the 1930s. They *both* established an untarnished record as spiritual healers. For forty years, until Ambrose died in 1972, the Worralls worked together to aid the sick. They both had consecrated their lives to God to be of service, and in countless cases, they found themselves the catalysts for true miracles of healing.

The Worralls concentrated much of their efforts on children, seeking to heal those little ones with twisted limbs, diseased organs, and hopeless prognoses. A great many of these children improved because of the healing sessions, and many were cured.

In the 1930s, when the Worralls began their ministry, they decided that they would not take any money for helping people. Ambrose worked during the day in order to pay for their expenses and the two of them would devote their spare time to helping the sick.

They told us about the rough time they had in being accepted by the church, which at the time took a very dim view of the approach the Worralls took in their healing services. "Somehow or other, theologians had forgotten that the very foundation of Christianity was built on the gifts of the spirit," Olga said.

Olga said that healing was a part of the original church; in fact, it was a mandate given by Jesus to go and heal the sick. The church was unsympathetic with the various gifts of the Holy Spirit, and at that time, the medical profession also had its suspicions of them as well.

Ambrose and Olga were not discouraged by the opposition. They only took a patient if he was given the proper medical attention or was under the care of a doctor.

In 1974, my husband Brad taped an interview with Olga just two years after her husband Ambrose died. A woman of remarkable strength, Olga carried on her healing ministry after her husband's death. She never ceased speaking of her husband as if he were still very much her active partner, and she continued to conduct the weekly healing service at the Mount Washington Methodist Church and to offer both her prayers and her healing energies to all those who came to her for help.

Brad asked Olga if she knew what it was that was supplying the patients with a cure that did not seem to come from medicine. Olga gave him some interesting insights, and they reveal the sincerity and love that was present in the Worralls:

Olga Worrall: "I don't know exactly. Perhaps we

somehow supplied that unknown extra ingredient that accelerates the normal healing process of the physical body.

"I don't know exactly what spiritual healing is. No one does. Maybe it's somehow akin to electricity. Of course, no one knows exactly what electricity is, either.

"Perhaps someday science will discover the law governing spiritual healing, and then it will be used as an adjunct to medical practice and will enable people to get well much faster."

Olga talked about how it took over forty years of plodding on and doing their work in spiritual healing, trying not to let the criticism bring in a negative dimension to their ministry. They kept their faith and belief in God rather than let man's *interpretation* of God in action dictate.

Olga and Ambrose never once talked as if the healing power was them, or that they themselves were the ones responsible for the healing. "Only *God* is able to heal whether He is working through a medical doctor or a clergyperson or any person who serves as a channel for the love and power of God's healing energy. Without God's power, you are utterly helpless."

⌒

Is prayer your steering wheel or your spare tire?—CORRIE TEN BOOM

⌒

Olga continued to say: "Now, even doctors are

more open to the idea of spiritual healing. I have met many doctors who are very compassionate people. I have even found that many medical people are themselves using spiritual healing. Many dedicated doctors pray for their skills to mend the body, but then there is that something extra that takes over and does the actual healing.

"The clergy, too, is now more aware of their responsibilities in the field of healing. I salute the Episcopalians, because they accepted the idea of the need to provide their people with a healing ministry and have healing services in many of their churches.

"I am in the Methodist church. We have been instrumental in keeping the New Life Clinic healing service going because of the healing successes demonstrated.

"Our healing services are ecumenical. Christians and non-Christians come together. We conduct a half-hour meditation and prayer time. It is in meditation that we listen and can hear the whisperings of God in answer to our prayers.

"Our healing service is conducted in a very dignified, very quiet way. When the people come to the rail for the laying on of hands, we don't ask them if they have been saved. We don't ask their denomination. Our business is to do the laying on of hands and to permit God to use us as a channel to bring healing into the life of that person.

"I feel that present-day spiritual healing has made a terrific impression on the lay person. If we can fill a church on a Thursday morning to overflowing with people who are there crying out for spiritual healing, this should be a sign to the churches to provide this type of ministry. People attend these services for soul healing as well as for physical healing.

"I feel people are 'soul sick' when they don't have communion with God. Their souls are crying out for this communion, and very often such soul sickness will be reflected in the physical body.

"If you can bring peace into people's minds, assure them that they are God's children, that God is concerned about their well-being, that those who have passed on ahead are very much alive and are eagerly awaiting their coming, that we do live after death, then, you can heal them and bring peace to their souls."

When asked her opinion of whether or not such spiritual healing can be developed, Olga's answer was:

"I don't think it is really possible to train spiritual healers as we can train medical doctors. Unless someone has the potential gift of spiritual healing lying dormant, the development of true, dedicated, spiritual healers would be very difficult. It seems that you either have the gift—or you don't. Of course, it is possible to help people refine the natural healing abilities that they do possess and teach them to use these faculties more effectively.

"I would suggest that every minister, doctor, and psychiatrist be taught to be aware of their gifts of the spirit and learn how to use these innate abilities fully and effectively.

"I would say that many people who have a desire to go into medicine are often natural-born spiritual healers. These persons heal without realizing it.

"In fact, I have found few dedicated doctors who were not true healers, but many of them cannot talk about their spiritual awareness because the medical profession is so opposed to unorthodox healing. These sincere doctors do, however, use their gifts 'sub rosa' and many of them have told me that they *pray* before very operation that they perform! I know many doctors who are truly holy people."

When asked how Olga knows what to do when she lays hands on people, and if it is intuitive, she said:

"Yes. You know *where* to put your hands. Certain states do not permit healers to place their hands below the shoulders as protection for unsuspecting people against unscrupulous false healers, and I approve. I have found that very often a mere hand clasp can heal the patient.

"I find that when people come to me and say, "please help me," their need triggers a force within me for healing, but if there isn't that immediate attunement, the energy may miss its mark. Compatibility is one of the several ingredients in spiritual healing. The healer and the patient must both adjust and continue trying until proper attunement is achieved.

"If I had my way, every church would have a developing circle of healers that would meet once a week under proper supervision. I have often made this suggestion and there is always some unenlightened soul who thinks all this is of the devil. Yet God's work will continue regardless of such thinking or opposition."

It so happened that through their perseverance, the Worralls both eventually *did* gain the respect of both the medical community and of many church officials. And I am sure that it was not only because of the extreme success ratio of healings, but because of their integrity as well that Olga was later researched.

The scientific experiments done through the NIH and NIE as well as by such noted scientists as Dr. Thelma Moss of UCLA's Neuropsychiatric Institute, among others, led to some fascinating breakthroughs. There definitely was a clear measurable change in various elements when Olga Worrall prayed over them. I was shown the results of test after test. An actual chemical change occurred. Even when the water that had been prayed over by Olga was used by another individual, other than Olga herself, to water plants, it was proven that the plants reacted as if there was some magic potion in the water that made them grow better.

This was utterly astounding. The implications of this led one to think again of the miracles of Jesus.

Chemically, he changed water into wine. Chemically, people who had been healed had their energy changed. Suddenly there was now the beginning of scientific validation for miracles. Suddenly, the myth of magic went poof in the light of modern research. When Jesus said to go forth and do the same, it still applies to us today not as wistful, wishful thinking, but a TRUE possibility!

Dr. Thelma Moss at UCLA used Kirlian photography, among other instrumentation, to evaluate and determine healing from Olga Worrall. Some terrific surprises came out on some of the first of the tests.

Olga was asked to pray over a leaf that had been injured. Olga did pray over it, but when the film was developed the leaf was not even there—it disappeared!

Dr. Moss said she was worried about how to tell this to Olga. But not coincidentally, Olga had a feeling and said she guessed she "gave it too much energy" on the first try and wanted to try again. Olga said she thought she knew what had happened, and she asked Dr. Moss if she could try the same experiment using the same leaf again the next day. She did.

This time the "aura" or the biomagnetic/electric field (as discussed in Chapter 5) showed Olga's incredible healing energy affecting the glow around the entire leaf—the whole leaf was missing!

In the words of Dr. Thelma Moss, ". . . This time, with more gentle treatment, the leaf flared brilliantly.

In other words, Olga Worrall was the first person we found who seemed able to direct the energy flow."

Of course, it goes without saying that the experiments were controlled, so that the proper precautions were undertaken to ensure their legitimacy.

~ 15 ~

The Power of a Prayer Group

In 1968–69, while on internship in a Lutheran church in Austin, Texas, my husband and I were fortunate to have the opportunity to meet Keith Miller. *The Taste of New Wine*, Keith's first book, has been instrumental from its first publication in 1965 in bringing about a great change in the church at large. Keith Miller had been extremely successful in business for many years, but obeyed a strong inner call of studying in seminary, and as director of Laity Lodge (an experimental lay conference center in Texas) and then completing work for a Ph.D. in psychological counseling.

One of Keith's greatest gifts to many has been his sensitivity to the need and desire of men and women for a genuine transformation by their faith, and his alertness to the fact that this did not seem to be happening in the institutional church.

～

For where two or three are gathered together
in my name, there am I in the midst of
them.—MATTHEW 18:20

～

Keith has inspired millions to find a very personal
relationship to God through prayer. "In their examination of the Scriptures as converted Christians, men
and women are discovering that institutional church-
manship, as it is commonly known in the United
States, simply does not express for them the wholeness of the new life they are experiencing." And as
he saw that people were rediscovering (as J. H. Old-
ham said in *Life Is Commitment*): "Religion is not a
form of experience existing separately from other
forms of experience. It is the transfiguration of the
whole of experience."

Keith dared to ask questions that a lot of us felt.
He noted that those who were on fire with the Spirit
of God found it nearly impossible to be satisfied to
"sit in a pew" or "to serve in a committee" and feel
spiritually fed. Keith advocated a call to honesty in
dealing with our individual lives spiritually.

This kind of honesty doesn't work out in the orga-
nized church because of the sheer numbers and the
size of a normal church congregation. Keith saw a
need to go back to meeting in small individual
groups, meeting in people's homes, just as the early
Christians did. He wasn't telling people to drop out
of church attendance or membership, but urged this

way of fellowship in meeting the needs of the "whole person"—body, mind, and soul.

At the time, I was already discontent with medicine, feeling that there was a strong need for recognizing the "Spirit" and the mind a well as the body for affective healing to take place. No one at the time I was in medicine supported my belief—in fact, the opposite.

I was beginning to see that theology-religion was just about the same. I saw and discussed the need in the ministry for recognizing the equal role of the mind and body in dealing effectively with parishioners. And a fast-growing feeling deep within me was feeding somewhat of a rebellious kind of attitude about the ministry in a "church." Jesus went out amongst the people—something that I felt was a strong need for the "church" to do, not wall out many who needed God the most because they had long hair or wore the wrong kind of clothes or had a different color of skin.

Clearly the scriptures say that Jesus was very specific about so many things that were not being adequately dealt with. "If you have ought against your brother . . . I tell you, go first to settle the matter *before* you go to temple." In other words, I was from the inside seeing and hearing the "gripes" and "grudges" that people had one against the other, and my understanding was that until we get the "inner" life and "every thought" straightened out, going to church to worship God is almost a hypocrisy. This, I knew, meant my inner life and every thought as well.

> You have heard that it was said to the men of old, "You shall not kill; and whosoever kills shall be liable to judgment." But I say to you that every one who is angry with his brother shall be liable to judgment; whoever insults his brother shall be liable to the council, and whoever says, "You fool!" shall be liable to the hell of fire. So if you are offering your gift at the altar, and there remember that your brother has something against you, leave your gift there before the altar and go; first be reconciled to your brother, and then come and offer your gift. Make friends quickly with your accuser, while you are going with him to court, lest your accuser hand you over to the judge, and the judge to the guard, and you be put in prison; truly, I say to you, you will never get out till you have paid the last penny.
> —MATTHEW 5:21–26

Jesus was, of course, not only talking about brother as in brother and sister. When he was asked who he meant by brother he said that all men were his brothers and all women were his sisters and the same goes for us. So, here again, to follow the exact teachings of Jesus, it is more important to be in touch with what we think, do, and say because we are accountable for each and every little thing we think, do, and say! He is really saying (forgive my paraphrase)— Forget about going to church if you think that is

going to make nice with the pastor, priest, or rabbi —
or God. Get right within yourself! Get right with
God! We are forewarned if you don't do it before
you die . . . you will pay for each and every little
thing that you did not take time to straighten out!

Now, looking at life from that perspective, it can
hardly be denied that priorities as a whole are all
mixed up in our every-day existence. The thing that
I found really exciting about these teachings is that
they are *the same* as most all other teachings. And we
truly are given a chance to repent each and every
day, not superficially, but with real depth and sincerity. We can't put one over on God: He knows our
hearts. The word "repent" literally means: to change
your mind, or to change your direction.

Group Dynamics
from a Flock of Geese

While I was writing the book, *The Mystery of Animal
Intelligence*, a friend sent me the following story by an
anonymous source. Nature often does give us such
beautiful illustrations of the unfolding of the Divine
in life which is all around us, if we slow down
enough to notice. (In lectures and workshops) I used
to use this same little story in the sixties and seventies for its wonderful message.

Follow the Lead of the Goose

Living where we do, near the Minnesota border, there are flocks and flocks of birds leaving to head south before the raw cold settles in. It has always been intriguing to me to observe the "V" formation that all birds take when flying somewhere particular. As each bird flaps its wings, it creates an uplift for the bird immediately following. By flying in "V" formation, the whole flock adds at least 71 percent greater flying range than if each bird flew on its own. How do they know these things?

Those people who share a common direction and sense a community can get where they are going more quickly and easily, because they are traveling on the thrust of one another!

Consider the wisdom of a goose:

When a goose falls out of formation, it suddenly feels the drag and resistance of trying to go it alone—and quickly gets back into formation to take advantage of the lifting power of the bird in front. If we have as much sense as a goose, we will stay in formation with those people who are headed the same way we are.

When the head goose gets tired, it rotates back in the wind and another goose flies point.

It is sensible to take turns doing demanding jobs, whether with people or with geese flying south.

Geese honk from behind to encourage those up front to keep up their speed.

What messages do we give when we honk from behind?

Finally—and this is important—when a goose gets sick or is wounded by gunshot, and falls out of formation, two other geese fall out with that goose and follow it down to lend help and protection. They stay with the fallen goose until it is able to fly or until it dies; and only *then* do they launch out on their own, or with another formation to catch up with their group.

If we have the sense of a goose, we will stand by each other like that!   —ANONYMOUS

The wisdom of a goose about the strength gained from sticking together one for all and all for one gives us an illustration of the support that can come from a group of individuals with the same commitment and desire—around any topic, actually, but in the context of prayer, the personal growth and strength from a group focused around prayer is exponential.

The power of Keith Miller's awareness in 1965, has come perhaps full circle and is even more evident today in the late '90s. The greater personal needs that people have that the church was or is not fulfilling was not so much condemning or chastising the church, but perhaps more so recognizing the sheer size of an average congregation prohibited the kind of sharing and caring that was desired. Also recognized is the responsibility of the individual and the family:

> The result is our churches are filled with people who outwardly look contented and at peace but inwardly are crying out for someone to love them . . . just as they are—confused, frustrated, often frightened, guilty, and often unable to communicate even within their own families. It is so easy to not notice anything wrong. But the other people in the church look so happy and contented that one seldom has the courage to admit his own deep needs before such a self-sufficient group as the average church meeting appears to be.
>
> > . . . *woe to him who is alone when he falls and has not another to lift him up.*—ECCLESIASTES 4:10

～ 16 ～

The Family Who Prayed Their Mom Back from the Brink of Death

Just last year I heard about a Milwaukee family who simply refused to give up on their mom. Medical specialists in the hospital urged the family to unplug her feeding tube and to permit her to die in peace. Although things looked very grim for forty-eight-year-old Rosemary Dietsch after an aneurysm burst in her brain and she went into a coma, her family rejected the doctors' quiet suggestion that they allow her to slip away from them.

Twenty-five-year-old Greg remembered vividly the shock that the Dietsch family sustained on that rainy early April afternoon when their personal physician, Dr. Dennis Ott, concurred with the specialists at the hospital.

"Dr. Ott told us that there was little or no hope that Mom would ever come out of the coma," he said. "If she ever did regain consciousness, he warned us, it would be on the level of a vegetable. She would never be able to recognize any of us ever again."

Robert Dietsch, fifty-four, put his arms around his three children—Greg, twenty-two-year-old Marc, and nineteen-year-old Terry—and, with his voice breaking and tears streaming down his cheeks, he told them that it had to be a family decision. He would not be the one to make such a major decision on his own in passing judgment on whether their mother would live or die.

Terry wiped her eyes on a tissue and uttered the words that came to be the family's credo. "Hey, Dad, guys, we've always been a praying and Bible-reading family that's put its trust in the Lord. I say we keep on praying until Mom is home with us and as good as new."

Marc nodded his agreement. "We'll make a joyful noise around her bed night and day."

"And we'll never stop praying!" Greg added.

From that moment on, there was always at least one member of the Dietsch family beside Rosemary's hospital bed.

Each day after work and on until the wee hours, Robert read the Bible with great feeling, just as if his beloved wife were awake and participating in their regular family Bible study.

Greg prayed aloud and placed his hands on his mother's head.

Marc, a sports enthusiast, assumed the role of a persistent coach. "Okay, Mom, come on now. I know you can hear me. Come back to us. Come back to us, Mom—right now. I know the angels probably want your beautiful love in heaven, but we're asking them to let you come back to us. We can't give you up!"

Terry, a gifted musician, played her guitar and sang all of her mother's favorite hymns, over and over again.

And at least once a day, all four members of the Dietsch family would form a circle around Rosemary's bed and clasp hands in a silent prayer for healing.

Within a week, an astounded nurse witnessed the impossible occurring when Rosemary opened one eye.

Three weeks later, both eyes opened and she looked around her hospital room.

The first week in June, just six weeks after an examination of the burst aneurysm had led experienced doctors to decide that Rosemary Dietsch would remain in a coma until death overtook her, she moved her fingers and toes.

In mid-July, less than three months after she lost consciousness, she was responding to sounds and recognizing members of her family. Her mouth moved as she tried to speak to her husband and children.

In another month, she was able to go home.

"Once Mom came home, she rapidly continued to improve," Marc said. "In just a little while she was able to walk and talk normally. Soon she was joining us in our prayers for her health to be completely restored. She ate meals with us, watched television, and began to read books, magazines, and newspapers."

By that Christmas, Rosemary Dietsch was once again able to play the piano and sing carols with the family.

"I know that I have been blessed with the greatest family in the world," Rosemary said. "They would not give up on me and they would not accept the doctors' analysis that I was doomed to live out my remaining days in a coma. Their love and their prayers activated God's great love and brought me back from the brink of death into a life even more glorious than before!"

~ 17 ~

Praying My Own Mom Back

In about 1982, I received a disturbing, surprise phone call from my grandma Johnson. She told me that my mom had been in a coma in the hospital, and the doctors had just told my dad that it didn't look good. In fact, they had just given the prognosis that she would most likely not come out of it alive. Grandma said, "The doctors told us that even if a great miracle occurred and Mom *did* come out of the coma, she would be brain-dead or severely brain damaged."

For a moment, I experienced double shock. I couldn't believe that Mom had been in a coma and I didn't even know about it; and, the "finality" of the opinion of the experts seemed beyond belief.

I asked Grandma if she was calling from home (which was Dearborn, Michigan). She told me she was calling from Mom's hospital room. When Dad called her, Grandma explained, telling of Mom's medical problems, she immediately left, and traveled to Schaumburg, Illinois (where my folks lived). Then, apparently several weeks later, Mom's condition worsened and she lapsed into a coma.

I lived in Virginia Beach, Virginia. I wondered if there would even be time to get to Illinois; then I realized with what the doctors had said that I would never get the chance to talk with my mother—ever again.

Twenty years earlier, while I was in nursing, I had spent time at some of the very worst institutions in the entire country, where there were "brain-dead, vegetable-state" patients. The sight was one of the most despairing, confusing, and hopeless of human conditions I had ever seen.

Even JESUS said: "By myself,
I can do nothing."

At that time, just about all human conditions and maladies greatly distressed me. Poverty, prejudice, injustice, wars, killing—these were all man-made conditions. But then one looks at the situations newborn babies worldwide are born into and how can that be just, fair, and equal? I was even struggling with my faith.

No matter how bad things had become before, I never lost faith (as I said, struggled—yes, give up on God, no). But this, the big one for me, *babies* born with terrible defects and deformities who were termed "vegetables," were put in these places to grow up—and for what? How could a loving God allow this? I questioned. Aren't babies supposed to be born into this world in innocence? God, why?

But then there were thousands of adults there who were vegetables. That didn't seem fair, either.

No matter what the instructors taught us, it didn't seem possible that these poor forgotten souls could not understand absolutely *anything*, so of course, no one even bothered. The patients were lucky to even be bathed and fed. It was devastating!

All of that came back to me, and in an instant I snapped out of my shock and had a firm conviction that no way was that going to happen to my mom! I always had a feeling that patients in comas and even the "vegetables" really might be able to hear and understand, under certain conditions and with a *lot* of love!

Somehow, as if all of those memories and questions I'd felt in the past mounted up to a strange testing point, I said a silent prayer. An immediate answer came: "She can hear you—talk to her, pray with her!" Now I felt *positive* that Mom would be able to hear me—no matter what the official verdict was!

Just to double-check and be sure that I heard correctly and understood, I asked Grandma if Mom was able to hear anything. Grandma said, "No, Little One (she always called me that), the doctors told us she was not aware of anything and would not be capable of hearing or sensing."

I told Grandma that I believed differently and asked her to hold the telephone earpiece up to Mom's ear for me while I talked with her. Grandma told me that would not do any good. I was extremely persistent, as I firmly said to Grandma that I didn't care, I just had to have her do that for me! After going back and forth a few times about it, Grandma finally complied.

When I was certain that Grandma was holding the phone to Mom's ear, I began to pray out loud. Then, talking directly to my Mother, I said, "Mom, I know you can hear me. The doctors say different, but you know me, I won't take their diagnosis over God's! I truly believe that you can hear me, and I know God is going to heal you."

Every so often, Grandma would take the phone back to tell me once again that there was no response from Mom; whereupon, I would ask her to please bear with me and keep on holding the phone to Mom's ear.

I kept this up, despite the protests and the passing of time. I continually told Mom how much I loved her, and how much she meant to so many people. Emphasizing the gifts I felt God had given her and that her time was not up yet, I would pray out loud and encourage Mom, by again repeating, "I know you hear me!"

Knowing that my parents had only recently come

to accept that my brother's death was suicide, not an accident as they had believed, I took risk by saying, "Mom, you know how empty you felt when Junior died. Me too. But, after losing Erik (my own son), think of me. I need you! Don't leave me!"

I have no idea what prompted me to get into that, other than something in my praying encouraged me to say that, and then to say: "Mom, please talk to me! Mom, can you hear me?"

Then I thought I heard a wee little response! ". . . yes, I can hear you, Sherry." Not sure if I trusted my own ears at that point, I yelled out, "Mom, mom, is that really you!" Again I heard her say, "Yes." What truly confirmed it for me was hearing Grandma yell for the doctor! We all thanked God. The miracle occurred—Mom was out of the coma, and NO brain damage!

18

Prayer Is Used in Therapy

Michael Elkin, a Massachusetts hypnotherapist and family therapist, turned to prayer while counseling an enraged and terrified woman. "None of the tricks I'd used with high-resistance, high-denial people worked," says Elkin. "Any time I tried to explain her experience, she'd respond with a level of rage that could peel the paint off walls."

Elkin did not abandon his normal techniques, but he began praying for fifteen minutes before the session he would have with this woman. "I would pray for the ability to keep my ego out of it, not to feel threatened, to see her as undamaged, and just be loving to her," he says. "I stopped trying to *do* anything. She became much more relaxed and pleasant. Since then, it's been a steady uphill climb."

⌒

The exercise of prayer, in those who
habitually exert it, must be regarded by us
doctors as the most adequate and normal of
all the pacifiers of the mind and calmers
of the nerves.—WILLIAM JAMES

⌒

Many traditional M.D.s are opening up to the
accumulated research on the *power of prayer*. Thus,
many hospitals are acknowledging the patient's request for prayer to be involved in their healing
process.

In his wonderful book, *Spontaneous Healing*, Dr.
Andrew Weil comments on religious healing:

A considerable body of research data supports the
beneficial effects of prayer on health. . . . It is reason-
able to think that belief on the part of patients is the
crucial factor here; however, some research shows
prayer to be effective even when sick people are
unaware that they are the objects of prayer, suggesting that unknown mechanisms might also be
at work.

⌒

Prayer is the greatest of spells, the best
healing of all remedies.
—THE YOSHT ZORASTRIANISM

⌒

There is a body/mind/emotion/spirit link. I have

championed this belief since way back in nursing school in the early sixties. No one else at the time was giving credence to that link—they accused me of having a few of my own links missing! But now that research supports the interaction of our states of mind/emotion/spirit on the body and vice versa, we have other things to muck up the waters. Pollution and radiation. There are all kinds of invisible rays zapping through our bodies and minds these days. We are just beginning to examine these effects on health and spirit. But none of us would argue with the "bugaboo guilt" placing restrictions on any of our states of being.

Saints and Cancer? Is Being Spiritual Hazardous to Your Health?

It is fascinating, though, that there seems to be a very definite link between cancer and the "saintly" personality. Dr. Weil says, "I reject the idea that people give themselves cancer by failing to express anger and other emotions, and I emphatically reject the notion that failure to heal represents any kind of judgment about a person's state of mind—or spirituality."

Dr. Larry Dossey is one of a few doctors who have looked into the relationship between prayer and healing. Dr. Dossey has thoroughly examined an interesting phenomenon of what does appear, on the surface anyway, to be a direct link between spirit and disease. Whether or not it is due to suppressed anger or emotions, or the sense of giving up something, more research needs to be done.

⌒

Science investigates; religion interprets.
Science gives man knowledge; religion
gives man wisdom which is control.
—MARTIN LUTHER KING, JR.

⌒

A remarkable 99 percent of 269 doctors recently surveyed said they were convinced that religious belief can heal. Dr. Herbert Benson, author of the book, *Timeless Healing*, said that doctors feel that strong because they have seen the power of belief. Dr. Benson's book offers scientific evidence that faith has helped to cure medical conditions. "We've seen that belief is powerful in conditions including angina pectoris, asthma, duodenal ulcers, congestive heart failure, diabetes, and all forms of pain. We see it all the time, and we can't deny it."

An amazing 75 percent of the doctors believe the prayers of others can help a patient's recovery. Thirty-eight percent said they think faith healers can make people well. Yankelovich Partners conducted the survey in October 1996, at a meeting of the American Academy of Family Physicians.

Dr. Benson acknowledged what a wonderful breakthrough this is that modern medicine is accepting these approaches.

He headed a Harvard Medical School conference on spirituality and healing in December 1996, as well as a conference, with another planned in the spring of 1997 for the West Coast.

━ 19 ━

The Master Prayer That Teaches Us How to Live— As Well As How to Pray

Matthew 6:5 tells us what Jesus said about prayer just before giving us the formula for prayer itself:

And when you pray, don't be like the hypocrites: for they love to pray standing in the synagogues and in the corners of the streets, that they may be seen of men. Verily I say unto you, They have their reward. But when you pray, go into your room and shut the door, pray to your Father, in secret, and thy Father, which sees you in secret, will reward you openly. But when ye pray, use not vain repetitions, as the heathen do; for they think that they shall be heard for their much speaking. Be not like them; for your

Father knows what things you have need of, before you ask him.

Then Jesus instructs them with a prayer that has been recited by billions of people around planet Earth for two thousand years. He then teaches them what has come to be called the Lord's Prayer.

Throughout the Gospels it is recorded that Jesus spent a great deal of time by himself to pray. It may not have been until late at night or early in the morning, at times, but one thing we know for sure is that this was a priority in his life.

At one point the disciples finally ask him, "Master, will you teach us to pray?" I found that one statement very interesting. The disciples had to ask him to teach them *how* (Luke 11:1). He tells them again about prayer. Jesus didn't invent prayer. Prayer is the foundation of all religions and faiths in some form or another. Jesus chose them to be his disciples, to study with him and to be the carriers of the message Jesus came to bring to the world. In a way, wouldn't one think that Jesus simply would have told them, "This is the way to pray"? He taught them a great many things. Why not *that*—until they asked?

Jesus let them come to the point that *the disciples felt in their own hearts that they really wanted to learn.* Prayer is communication with God. Didn't the disciples of Jesus communicate with God in some way *before* they learned this prayer? Of course they did, and they all prayed together as well.

Jesus was a radical in his time. If all that he taught was really put into action, it would be radical today as well. What was Jesus saying about prayer? In His day, religious laws were set. There were strict teachings about worship and all that worship involved, including prayer. Just about everything that Jesus taught was threatening the religious leaders of the day; especially those that ruled the Temple.

The Temple was the repository of all the knowledge about God, and only a handful were keepers of the keys. The Jewish Scriptures referred to the Law and the Prophets. Jesus made clear that his intention was not to destroy or take away in any way from the law. He merely said he came to fulfill and to explain the law to everyone. I think that was the problem. That was the job of the keepers of the keys.

Prayer had its rituals, as it does still today. I see nothing wrong with ritual, and I don't think Jesus did either, if I may be so presumptuous. But if it is ritual only and not deep-seated meaning and heartfelt, it misses the main point. Back then even healing was against the law on the Sabbath. Jesus gave the common people access to the understanding of the law, to healing, to direct communication with God.

Jesus said the people could pray anywhere anytime—*all* the time.

Jesus said it is not *how* a prayer is said or where it is said or what day of the week and how many times it was said that God cares about. Jesus said it is the sincerity and the depth of the prayer that God cares about most. Jesus stressed a deeper meaning to the law—for all people, not just to the religious leaders.

These were all major taboos. When Jesus spoke out as he did, basically telling the religious leaders that they were misleading the people, and telling the people that their salvation was in their own hands and not that of the rulers, he very much angered the law and the prophets.

When Jesus gave the Lord's Prayer, he gave all a simple formula of how to live our everyday lives and to fulfill that which we are meant to be—according to God's plan. Jesus did not take away a single law. He added to their understanding immensely. Not everyone liked his interpretation. As far as I am concerned, the example of Jesus himself and the interpretation He gave is what I believe as well, but it is the toughest of all.

I have always objected to taking any scripture from any reading out of context. You can always find another one that says something that seems to be opposite. To be fully understood, the whole picture must be viewed and understood. Yet when what Jesus said is put together, we realize why Jesus said, "Be ye perfect, as your Father is in Heaven."

Now that is, as we all know, seemingly impossible. To *be perfect?* Most of us know how short we fall of that command—daily. But that is what we are to *strive to be*—never giving up—because God never gives up on us!

The formula for doing that is to recite the Lord's Prayer. In order to explain why I am calling this the master prayer for life, I am going to divide the prayer into (six) parts and take each part at a time.

> Our Father,
> Which art in Heaven
> Hallowed be thy name

Jesus personalized God for the people. "Our Father" is our *Heavenly* Father as opposed to earthly father. "Abba" is the word Jesus was recorded as saying. God up until then had been any number of deities, such as the Greek gods and goddesses. The one God of the Jews was and still is hard to grasp. Seeing a personal God as Father and we as children brings to us an easier way for us to feel loved and cared for. A Father who loves all of his children also provides a reference point for us. God is the beginning. He was first and is the law-giver as well. Same as the Father was the head of household then, the provider of all things to his family. "Which" rather than Who is the original translation and is in fact closer in the meaning. "Which" is hard for us to understand because a personal father is a who. In this case it is more like spirit. In God and in spirit there is no male, no female, no north or south or east or west. God is everywhere, all places at the same time, and all-ruling, yet he is a Father-like provider and rule maker . . . and he loves us.

"In heaven" is the everywhere at the same time—all places, all times, all things, etc. The word from which heaven is translated means everything and all things that surround us.

"Hallowed Be Thy Name": This again means the omnipresence of God, the wholeness of God. The word *hallowed* comes from a root word that gives us the words hale, hearty, healthy, whole, heal—or holy and perfect.

This is what inspired me in the sixties that we were meant to be whole as holy beings, and that whole meant to look at body, mind, and spirit—not just spirit. So I formed a nonprofit center for that purpose. At the time it was considered by many to be blasphemous and against the church's teachings. Now it is becoming more understood, and commonplace even, that one has to view the body, mind, and spirit because they all work together as a part of a whole.

> Thy kingdom come,
> Thy will be done on Earth
> As it is in Heaven.

Not only should Thy kingdom come—meaning perfection, peace, harmony and total love wholeness—in us around us—but here on earth as well as God's kingdom in Heaven. As above, so below. Jesus is saying it is God's will for peace, harmony, love, and perfection. Wholeness exists in us here and now, but we all have to will it and do it before it can happen, unless there is divine intervention, as there has been in history and is prophesied for the future.

Give us this day our daily bread

The original meaning of this is not to ask God to provide food for us. It means to refer us back to the glory and the power of God—the supplier and provider of all things. And it is telling us that remember, God is the supreme Father and you are the inheritor of His supply, of His kingdom, of His creation. So the food is not just the bread for our stomach, but the air we breathe, the spirit of life within and without—the perfect. We are like a teaspoon of the water in the ocean of God life. And we are the only thinking and free beings God created here on earth. Free to have free will. Free to inherit a perfect kingdom as the inheritors. Obviously we do not live in a perfect world. But God provides the way for these provisions if you *trust* in *Him*. That doesn't mean He'll drop groceries from the sky every day, but the way is provided for *you*—for what you *need*, not what you might *want*.

Forgive us our debts as we have
also forgiven our debtors

This one part alone could clear just about everything up on the planet—if we all learned to forgive. This is clearly telling us that God's law has a qualifier. Jesus did not say, "Ask God to forgive you no matter what." He says plainly, ask God to forgive you as you have forgiven. So if you have anyone at all—in your family or among friends and acquaintances—for whom you harbor anger or malice, don't even think of getting "forgiven." It doesn't matter how many times you go to church in any given week, if there is someone you have not forgiven in your heart, don't expect God to forgive *you*. Plain and simple.

In many other places Jesus tells us that even if we have not killed anyone, we are in danger of hell fire if we are angry at someone. He even says not even to go to church (Temple) unless you first forgive and make things right that you have done wrong. Get right with your heart—your family, your friends—then you'll be right with God.

Ask yourself every day when you get up and every night when you go to sleep if there is something in your heart you need to make right. If there is some hurt that you have caused anyone or thing, make it right.

Lead us not into temptation
But deliver us from evil

This is more accurately translated, "leave us not" rather than "lead us not." We wouldn't think that God would deliberately lead us into evil. But then again, evil has its place in the scheme of things. "Leave us not" reminds us that there are definite temptations here on earth. I think Jesus was acknowledging that God realizes that and provides for us guardian angels and divine intervention. That is what I think Jesus was. He was divine intervention.

Today evil is rampant on Earth. Many people are not using their free will to love but to hurt. A good share of the healings that Jesus did were exorcisms. Jesus cast out the demons and allowed love and healing to be. Whether or not the demons are real demonic spirits or demonic actions, the point here is that if you sincerely want to be clean and want not to be evil, all you need to do is sincerely call on God's help to rescue you, and *He will deliver you* from it.

> For Thine is the kingdom
> And the power and the glory,
> forever and ever. Amen.

Even Jesus, who did fulfill the law and was obedient to the will of the Father, had to surrender to the will of the Father. "Not my will, But Thine Be done." The word *man* comes from a root word that means "thinking being," but the law of God is often beyond our understanding. It needs to be understood in spirit. God our Father who is all that we said above in the other parts of the prayer *is* the perfect presence and the perfect spirit. As Jesus said, "I can do nothing, except through the Father who is in Heaven." Neither can we. We can do nothing but through God the Father. Amen means, "and that's the way it really is," or that's the truth!

20

Mother Mary and Prayer

In our book, *Mother Mary Speaks To Us*, Brad and I wrote about many of the phenomenal and increasingly widespread appearances of and messages from the Blessed Mother of Jesus. We were struck by the numbers of people writing us from all over the world with similar sightings and teachings. I found one of the most interesting aspects of these messages to be that of prophecy. Mostly, Mary appeared to the "common" people. When they questioned why they were chosen, Mary's answer would indicate often that it was because of their sincerity and purity of heart.

The Blessed Mother Issues
Warnings for the Future

Annie Kirkwood, international best-selling author of *Mary's Message to the World*, told us how stunned she was when Mary started giving Annie messages to be shared with others. When Annie protested that she wasn't even Catholic, the Blessed Mother said, "Neither am I!"

Mary continued, "It is among the common folk that this message will spread, for all nations, all religions, and all people. The government officials are—as always—too caught up in their own importance to give thought to any other kind of life.'"

Annie says, "Mary comes this time not so much as her historical self, but as a nurturing maternal figure. She wants to remind the world that God is also loving as a mother is loving." Mary told Annie that she is appearing now because the earth and humankind are about to go through some major changes. "Humankind is about to take a dramatic evolutionary step forward . . . but we must prepare for a number of changes in our lives and in our planet."

Mother Mary told of approaching catastrophes that will actually move mountains and upturn oceans. Some new lands that were submerged will rise and some coastal regions will slide into the ocean. Earthquakes and volcanoes will be violently destructive and weather patterns globally will be altered. Annie told us that she didn't want to put the frightening prophecies in her book, she thought she would leave them out. But the Blessed Mother told Annie that "time was short, and people needed to be warned."

Pray, Pray, Pray for the World

Annie's husband, Byron, said they tried their best to inform people how to prepare for the coming changes in his book *Survival Guide for the New Millennium*. They both explained that again and again Mother Mary wants us to understand the power that we have available to us through prayer. Mother Mary tells us to "pray, pray, pray for the world." "She tells us that these predictions can be alleviated or lessened with prayer," Annie continued.

The reason Mother Mary wants us to know about these catastrophic events starting in 1996 and getting more intense toward 2000 is to make us aware that we need to make changes in our hearts and minds today. "She wants us to be *in continual prayer*, to be honest with ourselves, and not to delude ourselves into thinking that we are helpless," Annie explained. "We can foster great changes through prayer, but they will come as we foster the changes in our hearts and in our way of thinking."

In Annie's book, *Mary's Message of Hope*, the Blessed Mother tells us all: "As the representative of the divine maternal energy, I am available to all people. I will come to you with angels and with the love of God. Let your prayers be to God, but I am ever ready to help you connect to the Father."

Mother Mary Speaks of the Power of Prayer

Brenda Montgomery, a housewife living in Alabama, shared her experience with Mary with us. She was actually awakened from sleep with someone tapping her and, thinking it was her husband, she rolled over and saw that he was still sound asleep. What she did see changed her life forever. Mother Mary appeared in the brightest light imaginable. Brenda said, "I cannot tell you all the things that were going through my head—mostly feelings of inadequacy in the face of the Divine Mother. (Brenda, too, was a non-Catholic.) As she stood looking at me from behind the lace veil, I felt fear—and yet I felt completely open to her energy and her love and whatever was to come. My heart was pounding so hard, I thought once that I just might have a heart attack. And I knew that if I awakened my husband, the vision might be all over. So I remained very still and quiet. I just hung onto those sheets under my chin, barely breathed, and just watched."

Brenda said that she was just wondering why the Divine Mother had come to her when the following words crossed her mind, "Because you will share this information with many." At that, Brenda began to weep.

Now let us do something beautiful for God.—MOTHER TERESA

The Mother showed Brenda a TV-type screen on which she was given images of future events. "They came slowly, giving me enough time to see each one clearly and to put them all in my memory. They were pictures of alarming scenes of the massive destruction of cities." Mother Mary showed her things that she could do to prepare her household, like storing canned food, toilet paper, matches, medical supplies, candles, batteries, bleach, etc.

Brenda said that even Mary seemed to be weeping when she spoke with love about the importance and urgency of the next message.

"You must all pray to Christ, my son, to God the Father," Mary said, "You must pray for the Earth, the world, the people, the changing times—you must pray for them all."

"You must pray for healing. In prayer all things are possible. Even Mother Earth can be released from the torments of her changes. *Enough prayer can change the universe.* Prayer can bring rest to those souls who have passed to the Other Side.

"You must pray for all beings—good or bad. This is your duty to God.

"You may pray to me, and I shall guide your prayers to God if you choose. Set aside time to pray, as you would for meditation, and pray! Prayer must be done regularly—and in the total knowing that when a prayer goes out from you, it is received in the Light and given to God. The angels are there to guide your prayers to Christ, to God. Do not worry that your small prayer may be wasted upon a deaf ear. *Any* prayer lifted to the heavens will reach God.

"Human beings have not fully understood the power that prayer has. You must believe me when I say that prayer is the most powerful energy in the universe. It is your love magnified in Light.

"If you are not praying daily, begin to pray now! All prayers are heard. Prayer is the perfect healing for any pain, and discomfort. Prayer given in perfect love is positive power unleashed and used.

"Love the Earth with your prayers. Your future on Earth and in Heaven is defined by the amount of love-energy that you release in prayer. These are words of essence that hold truths beyond your understanding. However, in the demands of these days on Earth, you are to take this message and flow with it—and share it with others."

Mother Mary ended her message for all with: "I love you and pray for you—and it matters not whether or not you are Catholic, but that you are of pure spirituality and love. My love and peace goes out to you now—and I await; Earth awaits; the Christ, my son, awaits; God our Father awaits. Bless the world with your prayers."

—Mother Mary

Appendix

Prayers from Around the World

Prayers from Around the World: Index

Jewish   Prayer for all Mankind
Muslim Prayer
Muhammad's Prayer of Light
Three Shinto Prayers
Sioux Indian Prayer
Prayer from the Indian Vedas

As you will see from these prayers I have collected from around the world, some of which are hundreds, others thousands of years old, there is really little difference among us—even in what we pray for.

Africa

PRAYER FROM KENYA

LEAD US NOT INTO TEMPTATION

From the cowardice that dare not face new truth
From the laziness that is contented with half truth
From the arrogance that thinks it knows all truth,
Good Lord, deliver me.

Africa

Pygmies, Zaire

DEDICATING A BABY PRAYER

To Thee, the Creator, to thee, the Powerful,
I offer this fresh bud,
New fruit of the ancient tree.
Thou art the master, we thy children.
To thee, the Creator, to thee, the Powerful,
Khmvoum (God), Khmvoum,
I offer this new plant.

Africa

Prayer from Zaire

O thou Chief of Chiefs, we kneel before thee
in obedience and adoration.
Like the bird in the branches, we praise thy
heavenly glory.
Like the village sharpening stone, thou art always
available and never exhausted.
Remove we pray thee, our sins that hide thy face.
Thou knowest that we are poor and unlearned;
that we often work when hungry.

Send rain in due season for our gardens that our
food may not fail.

Protect us from the cold and danger by night.

Help us to keep in health that we may rejoice
in strength.

May our villages be filled with children.

Emancipate us from the fear of the fetish and the
witch doctor and from all manner of superstitions.

Save the people, especially the Christian boys and girls
in the villages, from the evil that surrounds them.

All this we ask in the name of Jesus Christ thy Son.

Buddhist Prayer

PANSIL (THE FIVE PRECEPTS)

I undertake the rule of training to refrain from killing
or harming living beings.

I undertake the rule of training to refrain from taking
what is not given.

I undertake the rule of training to refrain from
licentiousness in sensual pleasures.

I undertake the rule of training to refrain from
falsehood
and all wrong speech.

I undertake the rule of training to refrain from
drink or
drugs which dull the mind.

The Ten Perfections

I shall seek to develop the perfection of generosity, virtue, doing without, wisdom, energy, forbearance, truthfulness, resolution, love, serenity.

China

PRAYER FOR POOR LABORING FOLK

Humbly, simply, we come early, praise God's kindness,
  His great mercy.
Beg Him pity our distress, grant forgiveness for each
  trespass.
Bitter each day is our labor.
As we worship in this temple, fill our souls with His
  great peace.
Now we know God's grace will never cease.
Sometimes we bear pain and suffering till our
  hearts are full of darkness.
Father, never from us depart, keep us poor folk
  in your kind heart.
God, give grace to us and gladness,
Bring us joy despite our sadness.
May your mercy be our stay,
may your love enlighten each day.

Chao Tzu-ch'en

India

BUSY PRAYER

Like an ant on a stick both ends which
   are burning,
I go to and fro without knowing what to do
   and in great despair.
Like the inescapable shadow which follows
   me,
the dead weight of sin haunts me.
Graciously look upon me.
Thy love is my refuge.

India

PEACE PRAYER

May there be peace in the higher regions;
may there be peace in the firmament;
may there be peace on earth.
May the waters flow peacefully;
may the herbs and plants grow peaceful;
may all the divine powers bring unto us peace.
The supreme Lord is peace.
May we all be in peace, peace, and only peace;
and may that peace come unto each of us.

Shanti—Shanti—Shanti!
(peace—peace—peace)

THE VEDAS

Ireland

AN IRISH PRAYER

Guard for me my eyes, Jesus Son of Mary, lest seeing another's wealth make me covetous.

Guard for me my ears, lest they hearken to slander, lest they listen constantly to folly in the sinful world.

Guard for me my heart, O Christ, in thy love, lest I ponder wretchedly the desire of any iniquity.

Guard for me my hands, that they be not stretched out for quarrelling, that they may not, after that, practice shameful supplication.

Guard for me my feet upon the gentle earth of Ireland,
lest, bent on profitless errands, they abandon rest.

Japanese

THE PRAYER

Tensho-kotai-jingu yao-yorozu-no-kami
(Almighty God of the Universe and myriad angels)

Tenka taihei tenka taihei
(Peace in the world; Peace in the world)

Kokumin soro
ote tenchi no oki ni meshimasu ue wa
(When all people comply with the Will of God)

kanarazu sumi yoki mikuni wo atae tamae
(Give us a Heavenly Kingdom pleasant to live in)

rokkon-shojo rokkon-shojo
(Purification of the six basic emotions; Purification of
the six basic emotions)

rokkon-shojo naru ga yue ni
(Since the six basic emotions have been purified)

Kono inori no kanawazaru koto nashi
(It cannot be that this prayer will not be fulfilled)

Na-myo-ho-ren-ge-kyo
Na-myo-ho-ren-ge-kyo

Na-myo-ho-ren-ge-kyo (repeated)

Tensho-Kotai-Jingu-Kyo

Jewish

NEW YEAR PRAYER FOR ALL MANKIND

Our God and God of our fathers,
Reign over the whole universe in thy glory,
And in Thy splendor be exalted over all the earth.

Shine forth in the majesty of thy triumphant strength,
Over all the inhabitants of thy world.
That every form may know that Thou hast formed it,
And every creature understand that Thou hast cre-
ated it,
And that all that hath breath in its nostrils may say:

The Lord God of Israel is King
And his dominion ruleth over all.

Muslim Prayer

Our Father in heaven,
May Your name be sanctified;
Your commandment stretches over
    heaven and earth,
May Your compassion come upon earth
    as it is in heaven.
Forgive us our sin and wrongdoings,
You the Lord of all good things;
cause Your mercy to descend upon us,
Your healing upon this sickness,
    and it will be healed.

Hadith al-Rugya

Muhammad's

PRAYER OF LIGHT

Oh God,

Give me light in my heart
and light in my tongue
and light in all my body
and light before me
and light behind me.

Give me, I pray Thee,
light on my right hand
and light on my left hand
and light above me and
light beneath mine,

O Lord, increase light within me
and give me light and illuminate me.

Three Shinto Prayers

A Morning Prayer

I reverently speak in the presence of the Great Parent God:
I pray that this day, the whole day, as a child of God,
I may not be taken hold of by my own desire, but show for the divine glory by living a life of creativeness,
which shows forth the true individual.

An Evening Prayer

I reverently speak in the presence of the Great Parent God:
I give Thee grateful thanks that Thou hast enabled me to live this day, the whole day, in obedience to the excellent spirit of Thy ways.

A PRAYER FOR REPENTANCE

I reverently speak in the presence of the Great Parent God:
Grant Thy grace that in the matter of this egotism,
receiving Thy regulation,
no matter what it may be,
I may ever keep and perform it
and effect a change of mind.

Sioux Indian Prayer

Great Spirit . . .
Help me never to judge
another . . .
until I have walked two weeks in his moccasins.

Prayer from the Indian Vedas

May there be peace in the higher regions;
may there be peace in the firmament;
may there be peace on earth.
May the waters flow peacefully;
may the herbs and plants grow peacefully;
may all the divine powers bring unto us peace.

The supreme Lord is peace.

May we all be in peace, peace,
and only peace;
and may that peace come unto each of us.

Shanti—Shanti—Shanti! [Peace]

Enough prayer can change the universe.

For additional information on or about Steiger
books, tapes, products and workshops or to share
your own experiences—send a self-addressed,
stamped envelope to:
Sherry Hansen Steiger
P.O. Box 434
Forest City, Iowa 50436

SIGNET

INSPIRING TRUE STORIES

☐ **O. R.** *The True Story of 24 Hours in a Hospital Operating Room* by Pulitzer Prize-winner B. D. Colen. This gripping, minute-by-minute account of 24 hours in the operating rooms of North Shore University Hospital in Manhasset, New York, vividly portrays the mysterious world of the operating room, where a team of specialists perform one of scores of medical procedures. "A great book, terrific read."—Larry King
(179838—$4.99)

☐ **A ROCK AND A HARD PLACE** *One Boy's Triumphant Story* by Anthony Godby Johnson. The true life tale of a boy who refuses to succumb to bitterness and hate but believes in love, and who courageously fights to live, not merely survive—even after he is diagnosed with AIDS. "Harrowing!"—*Washington Post*
(181859—$4.99)

☐ **THE MOON IS BROKEN** by Eleanor Craig. This is the author's agonizing and intensely moving true story of her beloved daughter's emotional breakdown. A poignant, eloquently written, and deeply affecting account of a mother's wrenching heartbreak that could serve as a lesson in courage and commitment.
(173678—$4.99)

Prices slightly higher in Canada

SIGNET   (0451)

HEARTWARMING STORIES

☐ **EDGAR ALLAN by John Neufeld.** In this penetrating novel, John Neufeld examines the problems that arise when a white middle class family adopts a black child.   (167759—$3.99)

☐ **LISA, BRIGHT AND DARK by John Neufeld.** Lisa is slowly going mad but her symptoms, even an attempted suicide, fail to alert her parents or teachers to her illness. She finds compassion only from three girlfriends who band together to provide what they call "group therapy."   (166841—$4.99)

☐ **THEY CAGE THE ANIMALS AT NIGHT by Jennings Michael Burch.** A heart-wrenching autobiographical account of a child's odyssey through foster homes, orphanages, and institutions. He was a little boy who finally triumphed over loneliness to find the courage to reach out for love—and found it waiting for him.(159411—$4.99)

Prices slightly higher in Canada
